P9-CLP-588

DATE DUE

11/22/21			
3/11/22			

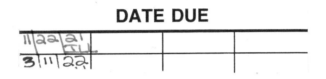

DISORDERS OF THE LOWER GENITO URINARY TRACT SERIES

SEXUAL DYSFUNCTION

FEMALE AND MALE PERSPECTIVES

A. R. MARKOS

Nova Science Publishers, Inc.
New York

NOTICE TO THE READER

The Publisher has taken reasonable care in the preparation of this book, but makes no expressed or implied warranty of any kind and assumes no responsibility for any errors or omissions. No liability is assumed for incidental or consequential damages in connection with or arising out of information contained in this book. The Publisher shall not be liable for any special, consequential, or exemplary damages resulting, in whole or in part, from the readers' use of, or reliance upon, this material. Any parts of this book based on government reports are so indicated and copyright is claimed for those parts to the extent applicable to compilations of such works.

Independent verification should be sought for any data, advice or recommendations contained in this book. In addition, no responsibility is assumed by the publisher for any injury and/or damage to persons or property arising from any methods, products, instructions, ideas or otherwise contained in this publication.

This publication is designed to provide accurate and authoritative information with regard to the subject matter covered herein. It is sold with the clear understanding that the Publisher is not engaged in rendering legal or any other professional services. If legal or any other expert assistance is required, the services of a competent person should be sought. FROM A DECLARATION OF PARTICIPANTS JOINTLY ADOPTED BY A COMMITTEE OF THE AMERICAN BAR ASSOCIATION AND A COMMITTEE OF PUBLISHERS.

Additional color graphics may be available in the e-book version of this book.

LIBRARY OF CONGRESS CATALOGING-IN-PUBLICATION DATA

Sexual dysfunction : female and male perspectives / editor, A.R. Markos.
    p. ; cm. -- (Disorders of the lower genito urinary tract series)
  Includes bibliographical references and index.
  ISBN 978-1-62100-781-4 (hardcover)
  I. Markos, A. R. II. Series: Disorders of the lower genito urinary tract series.
  [DNLM: 1. Sexual Dysfunction, Physiological--diagnosis. 2. Pelvic Pain--diagnosis. 3. Pelvic Pain--therapy. 4. Sexual Dysfunction, Physiological--therapy. WJ 709]

  362.196'8583--dc23
                                    2011038566

Published by Nova Science Publishers, Inc. † New York

Contents

Preface   vii

Introduction   ix

Part I: Sexual Function

Chapter I   Sex and Sexual Dysfunctions in History   1

Chapter II   The Sexual Response Cycle   13

Part II: Sexual Dysfunctions

Chapter III   Puberty, Sex and Sexual Dysfunctions   21

Chapter IV   Ageing, Sex and Sexual Dysfunctions   25

Chapter V   Classification of Sexual Dysfunctions   35

Chapter VI   Erectile Dysfunction (ED)   37

Chapter VII   Ejaculatory Dysfunctions   57

Chapter VIII   Peyronie's Disease (PD) and Acquired
                     Penile Curvature   65

Chapter IX   Priapism   69

Chapter X   Hypo-active Sexual Desire Disorder, Female
                     Orgasmic Disorders and Hyper-Sexuality   73

Chapter XI   Vaginismus, Sexual Aversion Disorder (SAD)
                     and Sexual Phobias   81

Chapter XII   Disease Induced Sexual Dysfunctions   87

Chapter XIII   Drug Induced Sexual Dysfunctions   **103**

Part III: Pain Disorders

Chapter XIV   Sexual, Genital and Pelvic Pain Disorders   **109**

Chapter XV   Dyspareunia: The Female and Male Prospective
                   and Management   **117**

Chapter XVI   Male Chronic Pelvic Pain Syndrome   **147**

Chapter XVII   Female Chronic Pelvic Pain Syndrome   **153**

Chapter XVIII Vulvodynia   **157**

Chapter XIX   Peno-Scroto-Dynia   **161**

Chapter XX   Urethral Pain Syndrome   **163**

Chapter XXI   Bladder Pain Syndrome and Interstitial Cystitis   **165**

Chapter XXII   Pudendal Nerve Entrapment   **171**

Chapter XXIII Pelvic Floor Dysfunction   **173**

Index   **175**

Preface

Sexual function is an integral part of human existence and wellbeing. Sexual dysfunctions could have detrimental repercussions on the individual, the couple, the family and society. During the course of clinical practice, the clinician will appreciate how a problem of one individual may have far reaching impact on the partner. The clinician will learn a great deal about the interpersonal dynamics between the couple from combined and separate interviews. The management of these problems, quite often, requires understanding, cooperation and involvement of the partner. The book "Sexual Dysfunctions: Female and Male Perspective" draws from these clinical skills to affect a better understanding and management of the dysfunction, as a problem for the couple; who need to take charge, responsibility and involvement in achieving its resolution. The clinician's guidance, throughout the process of history taking, clinical assessment, investigations and treatment plan, needs to focus on the couple as one unit; even at a time when either is attending the clinical assessment alone. With this perspective in mind, intimacy is an integral part of the sexual response cycle; which reflects on the interpersonal relationship of the couple and fabric of society. The clinician will identify that the management of physical issues is less challenging than emotional ones; although both are usually intertwined.

The book aims to provide individuals, couples and clinicians, who would like to understand sexual functions and dysfunctions, with a concise analysis of the different conditions and their management. The couple's better understanding of *the sexual response cycle* should underline their expectation, from oneself and the partner, during the course of sexual relationship and life long changes. This better understanding should foster a life long adaptation and balance between the partners; to affect better harmony and promote intimacy. In the case of a difficulty, the couple's understanding of the physiological basis of the problem is an important step towards its resolution.

Thanks to the efforts of dedicated scientists and clinicians, many of the sexual dysfunctions have a therapeutic approach, whilst others benefit from ongoing research. The clinician's sense of achievement, in managing a form of sexual dysfunction that benefited from pharmacotherapy, is challenged with other conditions that require extended behavioural therapy. With either scenario, the couple's achievement is rewarding for both patients and clinicians.

The author has taken due care to ensure that the listed drugs, dosages and routes of medication are correct. The prescribing physicians have duty to ensure the accuracy of the medication they prescribe and comply with their own clinical, professional, licensing, regulatory and statutory rules. Clinical, investigative and therapeutic procedures require training, experience, supervision, qualification, and accreditation. A practicing clinician must learn from the learned expertise of others and critically appraise the methods of his own choice.

Introduction

The World Health Organisation (WHO) recognised sexual health as a state of physical, emotional, mental and social wellbeing in relation to sexuality. Sexual health involves the enjoyment of sex; not merely the absence of disease, dysfunction or infirmity. It involves a positive and respectful approach to sexual relationships. It leads to pleasurable and safe sexual experience that is free of coercion, discrimination and/or harm.

Sexuality is part of the human experience that encompasses sex, gender identity, pleasure, intimacy and reproduction. Love, affection and intimacy contribute to the wellbeing of the individual and healthy relationship between partners. It can take place with or without sexual intercourse.

The medical community expressed late interest in the scientific understanding of sexual behaviour. Human sexual behaviour is influenced by complex factors; including personalities, attitudes, cultures, religious believes, social status, generations differences and/or drugs, weather recreational or therapeutic. Therefore, research into sexual function and dysfunctions is challenging and complex. The medical profession's better understanding of sexual function and dysfunctions should improve the clinical management of couples experiencing difficulties; by promoting evidence based practice.

Sexual dysfunctions (SD), deal with a range of disturbances in the sexual response cycle, which lead to personal and/or relationship difficulties. They include erectile dysfunctions, ejaculatory dysfunctions, sexual desire, pain and /or orgasmic disorders. They represent one facet of sexual health problems. Sexually transmitted infections, lower genito-urinary tract diseases, infertility, female and male pelvic disorders are other facets that impact on the sexual health of the individual and/or the partner. Sexual Dysfunctions should be clearly differentiated from Sexual Disorders; although nomenclatures are still at an early stage of evolution. Conditions like Sexual Sadism, Masochism, Paedophilia, Exhibitionism, Fetishism, Frotteurism and Gender Dysphoria are better recognised as *Sexual disorders and Paraphilias*; that fall within the territory of psychiatric sub-specialisation and outside the scope of this text.

The book aims to explore sexual function and dysfunctions, for both females and males. I will relate to cross speciality clinical expertise, to reach for a positive outcome. When "cure" is not available, I will reach for a clinical care pathway, to alleviate patients' distress and resolve clinical dilemmas. I intend to present a clinical practical approach; rather than mere exhaustive lists of conditions.

Part I: Sexual Function

Chapter I

Sex and Sexual Dysfunctions in History

Literature of love and sex existed since the beginning of recorded history. There are stark variations between literatures coming from old cultures and their reflections of sexual relationships. Certain cultures had explicit sexual literatures; and sometimes there are variations within the same ethnic group during different eras. Far Eastern history recorded sexual intimacies more explicitly, compared with that of the Europeans. For example, sex for the Taoist Chinese, as for the Hindu Indian, was a religious duty and a pleasurable way of improving the transmigration of souls. Chinese society considered sex as a private and personal matter, for the bed chamber; whilst in Indian society life was lived in public.

In *India*, the earlier religious writings considered sex as a private affair between the married couple, where both had a duty to please each other. Sexual literature (e.g. Texts of the 64 arts), was written for and kept by the upper castes and the religious orders, who can read. *Tantra*, a faith system that originated in India, asserts that sexual energy can be harnessed to achieve union with the divine. It represents an elaborate spiritual practice; one aspect of which is sexuality. The *Kama Sutra* is recognised widely as a literature on love and sex. It is thought to have originated some time between the 3rd and 5th Centuries; in India. Before the Kama Sutra, love figured very scarcely in sex literature. There were examples of writings on romantic love in early Egypt and Bawdy love in Greece. The Kama sutra gained notoriety as a book of physical interactions and sexual intercourse. This perception overlooked its extensive reference to the relationships between the partners and their interactions with the outside society. Interestingly, the text is subdivided into seven parts. One part only is devoted to the sexual union between the couple; whilst the other six relate to the interpersonal relationships and the couples' interactions with society. The Kama Sutra recognised four levels of love: love of mutual attraction, one-sided admiration, love of intercourse, and lastly, aspects of sex as kissing and embracing. The latter two levels relate to physical proficiency; the first two levels are driven by instinct, with no teacher or rules. The book identified seven kinds of sexual relationships, or "congress". Three were between true lovers: lovers who were accustomed to one another; two people whose love is in an early stage; and lovers who had long been separated. The next two kinds of congress are between two people who were both in love with someone else; and between a person and an unloved partner, transformed in imagination to the object of his desire. The last two kinds of congress are between a person from the upper class and a low class servant; or a peasant girl seduced by a man from a glamorous world. The text addressed the significance of difference in size between a man and a woman, in relation to the proportionate or disproportionate size of the genitalia. What are often overlooked in the publicity of the Kama Sutra are its detailed references to the different aspects of the interpersonal relationships, between a man and a woman; and their interaction with the surrounding society. It addresses the relationship with the religious order, worldly treasures and sensual pleasures. It calls for a balance between the attainment of virtues, wealth and love. The book recognises the influence of society on the couple, and the interaction, between both partners and the surrounding cultures. For example, a chapter is designated for the study of arts, another for the daily life of a citizen and amusements; including festivals, social gatherings, drinking parties and picnics. The *Ananga Ranga,* a less publicised Indian literature, is directed to attain fulfilment through physical and sensual interactions. It is thought to originate in the 15 or 16th Century. The text addresses the partner's general qualities, characteristics, temperaments. It refers to women from "various lands". It recognises the influence of social class, culture, physical build and behaviour on interpersonal relationships; and the consequent influence on consummating marriage and sexual relationships. Both, the Kama Sutra and Ananga Ranga represent advanced sex education manuals for the interpretation of sexual relationships in the Indian society.

The *Chinese* concepts of sexual relationships varied with religious beliefs and dynastic periods. In early China, the concept of creation, the vital essence and breath of life, known as *Ch-I,* has a supreme path, known as *Tao.* The elements of the world are in a continuing state of advance or retreat. Images of clouds metaphorically referred to woman's ovum and vaginal secretions; and rain to man's emission of semen. Taoism identified woman with an un-exhaustible supply of *Yin*. The man was identified with a limited supply of *Yang*. Taoism forbade men from using up their Yang essence without acquiring plenty of Yin essence; otherwise, health problems and death could be the outcome. Within this concept, nocturnal emission was a health problem; male masturbation or homosexual ties were forbidden as either practice would lead to the loss of *Yang* without achieving any *Yin*. Within the same concept, women had unlimited supply of *Yin* essence; therefore may engage in masturbation and homosexuality. Sex with a prostitute was thought to produce more *Yin*; and therefore acceptable. Red lamps, on the front door of wine houses, advertised their secondary business as brothels; which may represent the first concept of a "Red Light District". At the early centuries BC, Taoism records included sex manuals (e.g. *The Handbook of the Plain Girl and the Art of the Bed Chamber*). The later centuries experienced different cultures and ruling classes; with intermixing between Taoist, Confucian and Buddhist doctrines. *Taoist* doctrine, from the 6th Century onwards, returned with more sex manuals (e.g. *Secrets of the Jade Chamber*). Long, healthy and immortal life was thought to come from having many sexual relationships with many women and gaining their *Yin* essence. Sex was portrayed as a cure for man's ailments and different sexual positions were prescribed for certain ailments. The sex manuals, or handbooks, traditionally started with an introduction about the cosmic significance of the sexual encounter; then followed with recommendations about foreplay and description of the act of intercourse, including techniques and positions. In the following sections, the manual addressed the therapeutic value of sex and how to choose the right woman. The final section contained prescriptions and recipes. The instruction manuals had illustrations with pictures, as a source of bedside reference. To achieve ideal intercourse, the manuals described methods for maintaining erection and avoiding early ejaculation. For example, the "Jade Chamber" advised on pressing the area between the scrotum and the anus; an advice that is still in practice by some clinicians. Penile Jade rings were used, to maintain erection Some Chinese sex manuals correlated a higher number of women, with whom a man may have sexual intercourse, with greater benefits. The face-to-face position was accepted as the most natural and important one. There were no descriptions of Sadistic or Masochistic activities in the handbooks. Kissing in public was not acceptable. *Confucianism* led to authoritarian society, with legalistic and administrative controls and class distinction. The Confucianism culture put women at an inferior position to men; and men were allowed concubines. The sex act itself was only for procreation and the physical contact was confined to the bedroom. From the 12th Century onwards, the people subscribed to both, Taoism ruling their personal lives and Confucianism as a creed suitable for society and state. Tiny women's feet were a symbol of sexual desirability; which leads to foot binding, to force women to walk in a manner that strengthened the pelvic floor muscles. Women's legs became a symbol of erotic art. *Under Mongol rule*, China became a progressive puritan society. There was a Table of merits and demerits, which listed actions that would attract positive or negative points. For example, touching a woman's hand with lustful intent or telling a woman dirty stories would attract points of demerits. Women were prevented from taking their clothes off for medical care. In the 17th Century, the Chinese culture towards sex changed to what resembled Puritanical attitudes.

The *Babylonians and Assyrians worshiped Ishtar,* the goddess of love, fertility, nature, sex and war. Women celebrated victory with feasts and sex, at the Temple of Ishtar. Both men and women expected Ishtar to give them sexual power and fertility. With power shift to men, and the change of society from a matriarchy into patriarchy, the Temple of Ishtar became one of prostitutes. The rituals involved women sitting at the Temple after marriage, to have sex with a strange man, before consummating their own marriage. Men believed Ishtar would not listen to their plea unless they visited her temple and had sex with strange women.

In *Ancient Egypt* women enjoyed a social status, not rivalled in other cultures till recent history. Women had the right of inheritance of lands and properties. It was possible for a woman to divorce her husband. Society viewed adultery with contempt and considered it a capital crime. There was a strict regime of marriage for common people and punishment for those who broke the "The Marriage law". The man would be forced to divorce; but the woman was punished heavily. Polygamy and concubine were strictly forbidden to priests. Polygamy gradually gave way to monogamy, due to economic reasons and domestic harmony. Marital customs and sexual behaviours were different in nobility. There was a wide range, of acceptance or condemnation, according to the ruling class and time period. Pharaohs engaged in multiple marriages with foreign princesses, frequently for political and diplomatic reasons. The limited old Egyptian language on kinship led to the wrong perception that incest was rife in ancient Egypt. The term used to refer to the actual father will also refer to male ancestors or a grandfather; whilst "sister" may refer to "beloved", wife, mistress, lover, concubine, niece or aunt. As royal blood ran through females, to become a pharaoh the man had to marry a Royal Princess; who could be his sister or half-sister, within the fore mentioned remits. It was forbidden to enter a temple after intercourse, without washing. Sexual intercourse was prohibited and avoided in temples and tombs; contrary to eastern cultures. There is no indication in Egyptian history for the existence of "temple prostitution"; which was part of temple worship in surrounding cultures. According to the ancient Egyptian belief, life after death is a continuation of life on earth and sex was part of it. Gods had sex in ancient Egypt. The god of earth and the goddess of night sky were in a state of love-making, but separated later by the god of air. There is scarce pornographic material depicting homosexuality; which is not surprising since "The book of death" prohibited homosexual acts. Other papyri forbade homosexual acts between women. There are engravings of women touching and embracing each other in a banquet and surrounded with female dancers and musicians. This reflects a culture of women socialising and entertaining together, whilst shunning public or erotic stimulation of men.

Ancient Greece and Rome were patrilineal societies, where men owned everything including women, property and slaves. Women were clothed and veiled, not educated and had no rights in marriage. Greek society viewed rape as an expression of domination; with men preying on women at water wells. The cult of Zeus entailed god raping women. Society considered this cult teaching acceptable. Women were not allowed to walk alone, fearing rape. The Greek men considered prostitutes for pleasure, concubines for daily needs and wives for bearing legitimate children. Women were not expected to commit adultery. They also drove a difference between homosexuality within a relationship, when men had sex clothed, contrary to having sex with a homosexual male prostitute, which was depicted naked. Most of the male lovers were young, aged twelve to fourteen. Phallic replicas were used in temples and paraded in religious cults as a symbol of fertility. Roman women married younger, at the age of twelve. Greek women married at the age of sixteen and Spartans at eighteen. In Roman and Greek history, Venus and Aphrodite were equivalent goddesses to Ishtar. At times, Roman social pressures operated against marriage, family life and production of children; which lead legislations against celibacy. The combination of lead poisoning from water pipes, chronic alcoholism and early death rates, led to a decline in fertility and productivity. There were three forms of marriage in the ancient Roman society. The first was highly ceremonious and difficult to dissolve; the second had a resemblance to bride purchase, with several ceremonies. In both forms, the bride was passed from the possession of her father to that of her husband. The third is a trial marriage that is legally binding after a year of continuous association with her potential husband. During the trial year, the woman continued to be a member of her father's family. *Ars Amatoria* is a first Century roman manual, on the art of flirtation; contrary to the meaning of its title: The Art of Sex. Similar Chinese sex manuals were more concerned with what happened inside the bed chamber; whilst Ars Amatoria with how to reach there. The Kama Sutra addressed both issues, with wider social perspectives. *Socrates* captured the mind of the early Greeks in saying "women are by no means inferior to men, all they need is a little more physical strength and energy of mind". Greek women's political and legal rights were only equivalent to those of slaves. The male next of kin had absolute authority on females. Women received no education, were not allowed to go out un-chaperoned or be acquainted with men except their husbands and the close male relatives. Society limited women's social interactions. On the contrary, men spent more time interacting socially with prostitutes; some of whom grasped knowledge, literature, accounting and politics. They named them "*hetaerae*". Concubines had a lower social status; with no expectation of literacy or knowledge. Greek men kept concubines as secondary bed partners for their "daily needs". The convenience of using brothel girls later replaced the tradition of keeping concubines at home. Brothels flourished in towns encountering travellers (e.g. ports). The worship of Aphrodite involved sex with temple prostitutes. People attempts to please the gods involved the dedication of women to the temple of Aphrodite, to act as hetaerae, who used both her body and mind to entertain the worshipers. Socrates captured the mind of the early Greeks in saying "women are by no means inferior to men, all they need is a little more physical strength and energy of mind". Greek women's political and legal rights were only equivalent to those of slaves. The male next of kin had absolute authority on females. Women received no education, were not allowed to go out un-chaperoned or be acquainted with men except their husbands and the close male relatives. Society limited women's social interactions. On the contrary, men spent more time interacting socially with prostitutes; some of whom grasped knowledge, literature, accounting and politics. They named them "hetaerae". Concubines had a lower social status; with no expectation of literacy or knowledge. Some Greek men kept concubines, as secondary wives, for their "daily needs". The convenience of using brothel girls replaced the tradition of keeping concubines at home. Brothels flourished in towns encountering travellers (e.g. ports). The worship of Aphrodite involved sex with temple prostitutes. People attempts to please the gods involved the dedication of women to the temple of Aphrodite, to act as hetaerae, who used both body and mind to entertain the worshipers.

In *medieval Europe*, the man-woman relationship was influenced by men's absence, on long-term wars; which promoted the need for women's safety and the need for the chastity belt. It was constructed of a metal waist girdle, a front to back framework, with two openings for urination and defecation; but preventing penetration. The girdle was locked with a key; which ignited humorous stories of duplicate keys . It is thought that the belt was invented first to protect women against rape, and continued to be used up to the Eighteenth Century, to protect the woman from masturbation. Women were left in charge of the family estates and taxes. For practical reasons, they had to appear in front of authorities and courts. This promoted a different position of women in society and the sexual relationships of partners. The church's disapproval to divorce and appearance in society of stories of "courtly love" changed the woman's status in society into a "lady". Courtesy books appeared; to educate men on how to behave in a "civilised manner". Allegory and poems of love flourished during this period. Chivalry became the aspiration of men, virtue and chastity of women. This status did not infiltrate throughout society into commoners, but was rather a goal and aspiration. Mistresses were a normal occurrence in European aristocratic families. Historians refer to the Fifteenth Century as the age of bastards. Aristocratic families treated them as part of the household, cared for by money, never inherited land and became legitimate children, if the parents were later married. In England, they continued to be illegitimate; well until the 1960s. In English aristocracy, the idea of a mistress was not generally accepted, as in Europe; as the household services were provided by servants and the sexual services by prostitutes. Brothels were part of the expansion of cities. There was a prevailing ideology that "prohibiting prostitution would lead to polluting the whole society". During the Renaissance, prostitutes serving the higher society were expected to sing, play instruments and recite poems; similar to the role of the hetaerae in Greece; and their fees reflected their high life. Other intermediary outlets for sexual liaison (e.g. Bath houses) were widespread in Europe and were known in England as "Stews". Their designs depended on the status of the visitors. Baths to accommodate half a dozen people, in a vertical position, were the norm. Baths for a horizontal position, with attached dry rooms and beds for massage, were available for a higher fee. Church registers and court records listed hundreds of cases of adultery. There were outbreaks of sexually transmitted infections. The spread of Syphilis, in the Sixteenth Century, revived the blame culture between European nations. The

Germans called Syphilis the "Spanish Scabies", the French called it "Neapolitan Malady" and the Spaniards "French Disease". The timing of its appearance, following the discoveries of new worlds, has led some historians to consider Syphilis an "imported" ailment; as the epidemic coincided with the return of sailors from the overseas voyages.

The period of *Reformation and the Counter Reformation in Europe*, reshaped the man-woman relationship. Celibacy and vows of continence were no longer a standard to measure up to. Marriage and sex was seen as an outlet for frustrations, otherwise perpetuated by active chastity. The marriage contract for life, under the Catholic Church, was challenged by the alternative option of separation without remarrying under the Reformists. Regulating matrimonial laws became the responsibility of civil powers. The sexual relationship extended its dimension from procreation into sexual fulfilment for each of the partner's needs and avoidance of extra-marital relationships. Extra-marital activity was unacceptable. There were social variations and extremes. For example, the "Puritans" went the whole way into segregating their families and lived in closed communities. They flogged those who they judged as "fornicators or adulterers"; who they named and shamed.

Interventions to produce sexual changes were practiced through-out history and in different cultures. Some of the interventions had no scientific basis and others lead to harmful effects that reached toxicity. The practice of *castration* is a good example. The sheer number of *eunuchs* led their count, at times, as a "third sex". Turkish and Middle Eastern cultures considered the eunuchs' suppressed sexual potency and inability to father children, a safeguard for their position as house servants and guards for the "harems". In Rome and China, the eunuchs were kept in the house for their youthful appearance or as sex subjects. The eunuch's lack of dynastic opportunities and sexual persuasions promoted their position as civil servants and public figures. They were not considered a threat to the royal order or house-hold. The Assyrian and Persian empires kept eunuchs in all court posts. At periods of Chinese history, the order of "Eunuchs" achieved a powerful status. The Chinese emperors kept as many "male favourites" as female partners and wifes. Some Turkish rulers kept female eunuchs. In the 16th and 17th Century, there was a practice of castrating boys before reaching puberty, to retain their effeminate voice, for operatic singing (i.e. Castrato). The practice of castration was banned by various Roman emperors and later by the Church.

The Chinese were able to *extract sex hormones* from urine, by a process of evaporation, distillation and crystallization. They used the extract for the treatment of impotence and to stimulate beard development.

The idea of a *male condom,* made of animal intestine, is thought to have been introduced first by the Romans. Other accounts suggest a Persian origin; from the word Kondu, which described a storage vessel made of intestine. *Female condoms,* made of goat's bladder, were also described. The Condom's primary function was to avoid pregnancy. A sixteenth century Italian anatomist invented a *linen penile sheath*, to avoid the acquisition of syphilis.

Oral contraceptives were known in some ancient South American cultures. Cherokee women considered that chewing and swallowing the roots of spotted cow- bean plant can induce sterility. Paraguayan weeds were also used to reduce fertility. The practice of inserting *materials in the upper vagina* for contraception was practiced widely between Ancient Egyptians, Romans and Greeks. Olive oil, oil of cedar, ointment of lead, lemon juice, frankincense and/or many other herbal preparations are examples of materials that were used alone or in combination to avoid pregnancy. Sponges were used to absorb semen, oily materials to hinder the progression of sperms and acidic materials to kill them. Women from different cultures realized that continuing breast feeding reduce fertility; which they used to space the time between pregnancies. Byzantine writings described a natural *safe period* at the beginning and end of the menstrual cycle and advised men to wash their genitals in vinegar, which has a strong spermicidal effect.

Pregnancy tests were described by the Ancient Egyptians. A Thirteenth Century papyrus advised the woman, who was concerned with her pregnancy status, to urinate daily on bags containing grains of wheat and barley. A pregnant woman's urine was expected to accelerate the grain's growth. Babylonian midwives used tampons soaked with plant extracts, to be inserted into the vagina of a woman requesting a pregnancy test. A colour change, after 3 days of abstinence from sexual intercourse, was used as an indication of pregnancy. The colour change could be the result of a change in vaginal acidity associated with pregnancy.

The ancient Egyptians described *impotence* as "weakness of the male member". They used potions, oral drugs and local remedies applied to the penis, to treat impotence. They relied on magical spells, to support their remedies. They described *persistent erection*, in association with "diseases of the cervical vertebrae that lead to upper and lower limb paralysis". They practiced *circumcision*; but not on all males. There is evidence that they performed circumcision on boys, adolescents and men; but their purpose is not clear.

The Chinese concept of loss of yang by any indiscriminate loss of semen led them to develop explicit methods and practices to *delay ejaculation*. The practices involved the concentration of thoughts, closed eyes, deep slow breathing, arched back and stretched neck. Some sex therapists continue to advice techniques for the management of *pre-mature ejaculation.*

Aphrodisiacs were known throughout history and almost in all cultures. The range of products was wide and diverse; and users claimed success, even with the simplest of recipes. Oysters, for example, gained and continue to have a wide reputation, but scientific evidence is difficult to come by. The Romans believed that the Spanish fly have aphrodisiac properties. Augustus Caesar's wife slipped the Spanish fly into imperial family food, to induce sexual indiscretions. The Greeks regarded muscles, crabs, snails, honey, eggs and onions as aphrodisiacs. Erotic ointments and aphrodisiac wine were known to Romans. Satyrion, a plant with erect stem, double root and red leaves; was considered by both the Greeks and Romans as aphrodisiac; when added to wine or simply when held in the hand. Another remedy was thought to be effective by its mere placing under the bed. In the Ancient East, aphrodisiacs came in recipes that came in the form of pills or potions. The Chinese physician's secret collections of prescriptions describe four recipes for the different seasons of the year. A love manual, named "Guidelines of the Jade Room" described powders for topical application. on the penis or inside the vagina. Middle Eastern manuscripts describe aphrodisiacs for women and others for men. The mandrake had a wide spread reputation that persisted for a long era and culminating into strict rituals for harvesting the plant. It contains Atropine and Hyoscine, to induce initial excitement followed by sedation and hallucination. The effect of opium, in inducing relaxation and heightened enjoyment of sensual pleasures, had been exploited by different cultures. Far Eastern and other cultures continue to exploit the effect of ginseng as aphrodisiac. An Indian recipe of powdered white thorn apple, pepper and honey, was rubbed into the penis, to induce irritation, vaso-dilatation and erection. Its consequent contact with the female genitalia during fore-play, would have lead to vulval and clitoral irritation and increased sexual arousal. There were other wide spread strange practices used by different cultures; like whipping the genitals with stinging nettles, eating large amounts of onions and cress, cabbage steeped in goat's milk and carrots. Assyrian's use of love spells and application of iron fillings on the female genitalia show the extremes which people were prepared to undertake to improve their sexual potency.

Sex toys were widespread in different ancient cultures. The Greeks depicted Dildos on vases and mentioned them in literature. One Greek short comedy explained how one Dildo was passed between neighbours. Another comedy show how the manufacturer of Dildos kept his business in secret to avoid paying tax. A Tenth century AC Byzantine encyclopaedia described the Dildo as a "leather phallus used by widows and lesbians". Indian love manuals promoted the use of penile prosthesis, to assist a man who is married to an "elephant woman". The manuals suggested the use of a hollow tube that is strapped to the waste with strings. The tubes were made of metals, reeds softened with oil, wood, buffalo horns or ivory. Chinese texts described Dildos, made of ivory or wood and their popularity between lesbians. They warned against their excessive use and depicted the possible damage to internal organs. They described plants that they inserted into the vagina for sexual gratification; due to the plants' affinity for the absorption of fluids, swelling and enlargement inside the vagina.

The idea of *diseases transmitted by sexual intercourse* appeared in Chinese literature as early as the 7th or 8th Century AD; but far behind Egyptian papyri. Both observed a relationship between multiplicity of sexual partners and transmission of certain diseases. The Chinese identified syphilis in the beginning of the 16th Century and used their observations to warn men against prostitutes.

Chapter II

The Sexual Response Cycle

The Sexual Response Cycle

- Desire Phase
- Arousal and Excitement Phase
- Plateau Phase
- Orgasmic Phase
- Resolution Phase
- Refractory Phase
- Satisfaction and Intimacy

The sexual response cycle is the sequence of physiological, physical and emotional changes that take place during sexual activity. It involves a positive feed back mechanism between the genitalia and the brain. The erotic stimulation of one sends neural signals that promote sexual arousal of the other. Knowledge of the physiological changes should help individuals and therapists to identify the underlying type and cause of sexual dysfunction, to promote its prevention and plane a practical treatment strategy. Both women and men experience desire, excitement, plateau, orgasm and resolution phases. Men experience an additional refractory phase; which does not affects women. The sexual interaction between the partners contributes into intimacy; which is an important aspect of the human sexual relationship.

The timing of each phase differs between genders, age groups, individuals and partnerships. The intensity of response and length of each phase also varies between individuals. The better understanding of the partners, of each others sexual functions and responses, can help to avoid dysfunctions. In case of difficulty, the understanding of the sexual response cycle could be used as the basis of promoting effective therapy and enhancing the sexual experience. The couple need to view the sexual response cycle as series of sequential inter-related events that requires harmony between the couple; and leading to personal satisfaction, bond, intimacy and possibly procreation. The better analysis and identification of elements of dysfunction of the sexual response cycle, should help couples and therapists to plan the management care pathway.

The ventro-medial nucleus (VMN) of the hypothalamus is the main brain area that controls female sexual behaviour. The preoptic area is the principal area controlling male sexual behaviour; which has a reciprocal connection with VMN of the hypothalamus. The two areas are interconnected with other regions of the cortex, amygdala and spinal cord. The sex related neural network is responsive to gonadal steroids. Initial stimulation takes place during a specific period of foetal development; which promotes glial, dendritic and synaptic numbers and density. This network is responsive to adult alteration in gonadal steroids.

The *desire phase* is influenced by physical and psychological drives. The physical drive is the biological drive which is influenced by age, general health and hormonal balances. In both women and men, desire requires well balanced neurotransmitters, testosterone and dopamine levels. Testosterone levels increase in females in the mornings, pre-ovulatory period, when in deep romantic love and after moderate alcohol intake, in men, it is higher in the morning, during summer and autumn and during attempts for conception. The psychological drive is the motivation to have sex; which is influenced by mood, physical attraction, interpersonal relationships and past experience. Sexual desire may be initiated by memory, fantasy, and/or sensual stimuli. It is influenced by social and cultural factors. It may lead to a cascade of stronger want for sexual stimulation. Individual's reactions to stimuli are idiosyncratic and reflect the persons own thoughts, feelings and experiences. Desire is a prelude to sexual excitement and sexual activity. It may not progress without further mental or and/or physical stimulation. Sexual arousal in females follows erotic stimuli. For some it may require a visual stimulus; whilst others require intimacy, physical touching, caressing and perhaps mental fantasising. The person's own *appetite for sex* underlines his/her sexual desire. There are wide personal variations and inter-personal positive, neutral or negative cues. The appetite for sex could be described as *global and general or situational and specific*. The general desire for sex bears similarity to appetite for food. It reflects the individual's global experience of desire for sex; irrespective of the partner or stimulus. Situational and specific desire of sex relate to an individual or circumstances. It resembles the desire for one food or dislike of another. The Intensity of an individual's desire for sex bears similarities to appetite for food. A large proportion of the population falls within a middle average. A small proportion of the population has high sex desire; whilst another has a low or no desire for sex. This bears similarity to the appetite for food, with cases of Bulimia on one end of the spectrum and Anorexia on the other.

Sexual Desire problems pose a challenge for clinicians in its management. Contrary to Erectile Dysfunction (ED), there is no acknowledged or licensed drug therapy that is supported with scientific evidence. This does not preclude the need for resolution, by addressing personal and inter-relationship dynamics between the couple that may have influenced the sexual desire and will affect its management.

The sexual desire of a male patient suffering with ED, and/or that of his partner, could be substantially improved on treating ED. The male patient's fear and/or anxiety of ED could have a negative effect on his desire. The partner's build up of frustrations will reflect negatively on her desire for sex, fearing another episode of disappointment. The woman's perception of the negative effects of ED on her partner is bound to reduce her desire.

The *Arousal and excitement phase* is a response to sexual thoughts or activities. It extends from the point of arousal to the highest point of excitement. The duration varies between individuals and can last from a few minutes to several hours. This phase may be repeated several times before a plateau is achieved. It requires adequate mood, brain and/or genital stimulation; in both sexes. It involves brain centres, which require testosterone; and genital excitement, which require adequate innervations, circulation and cavernousal function. It is characterised with muscle tension, increase in heart and respiratory rates. In females, there is hyperaemia of chest, neck and back skin and erection of nipples. There is increase in genital blood flow in both sexes; which leads to clitoral and labial swelling in females and erection in males. In males, this is followed by scrotal tightening and elevation of the testicles and secretion from the Cowper's glands. In females, the changes are followed by increase in vaginal transudate, breast fullness and swelling of the vaginal wall. The increase in vaginal transudate takes place within 10 seconds; but may take longer in some women and during lying down. The vaginal transudate is a plasma fluid mixed with vaginal mucus;

which facilitates lubrication and prepares the vagina for penetration. It is mediated by the release of Vasoactive Intestinal Polypeptide (VIP).

The early phases of the sexual response cycle are controlled mainly by the para sympathetic autonomic nervous system. Stimulation of the sympathetic system (e.g. anxiety, apprehension, pain and/or stress) may interrupt the response cycle; due to dominance of the sympathetic system. Clinically, this may present as problems in achieving or maintaining erection or lack of vaginal lubrication. The vaginal transudate may remain entirely intra-vaginally with the vulvo-vaginal introitous remaining dry; leading one or both partners to the erroneous assumption that arousal did not take place. Increased clitoral hypersensitivity with excitement is a natural response aimed to promote the cessation of foreplay and the consummation of intercourse. Ignoring the clitoral hypersensitivity response, by either or both partners in persuasion of direct stimulation, can lead the woman to experience pain and consequently interrupt the response cycle.

The speed and intensity of the excitement phase varies between individuals and in the same individual between sexual experiences. Recent pharmacological studies indicate that adrenergic blockade, calcium channel blockade and other unknown mechanisms contribute to erection. Studies of these mechanisms can contribute to improvement in the understanding of sexual dysfunctions' therapeutics.

The *plateau phase* follows with intensification of changes that took place during excitement. The increased genital blood flow intensifies erection and turgidity in males. In females, the vaginal wall continues to swell and become dark purple. Clitoral sensitivity intensifies and eventually the clitoris retracts under the clitoral hood, to avoid direct touch. In both sexes, respiratory rate, heart rates and blood pressure continue to increase. Muscle tension increases and may culminate to spasm in hands, feet and facial muscles.

The increased clitoral sensitivity circumvents continuation of foreplay and promotes intercourse. Continued stimulation of the clitoris during this stage of hypersensitivity, may lead to pain rather than pleasure. The withdrawal of the clitoris under its hood could be wrongly perceived by the partner as cessation of response to arousal.

The *orgasmic phase* is short, lasting for a few seconds, and is characterised by the sudden release of sexual tension. The majority of women are able to have sequence of orgasms without a refractory period. The majority of men experience a refractory period during which they are not able to achieve another orgasm. Penile stimulation can lead to orgasm in nearly all men; whilst few respond to prostate and/or nipple stimulation. Clitorial stimulation produces orgasm in most women. Cervical, anterior vaginal wall, breasts and/or nipple stimulation lead to orgasm in some women. Both men and women have nocturnal orgasm. It requires spinal thoracic, lumbar, sacral centres (T12-L2 and S2-4) and brain connections and dopamine-serotonin balance. The blood pressure, respiratory and heart rates are at their height. There are involuntary muscular contractions and spasms of feet muscles. Rhythmic contractions of the muscles surrounding the base of the penis (bulbo-cavernosous) result in ejaculation. Similar rhythmic contractions take place at the muscles surrounding the lower end of the vagina; which constricts and massages the penile base during intercourse. The uterus lowers into the upper vagina, which locates the cervix in a favourable position for direct contact with semen ejaculated into the vaginal vault, which improves the chances of sperm access to the cervical canal. The cervical canal opens to facilitate transfer of sperms into the uterine cavity. The cervical opening continues for some 30 minutes following orgasm. The pelvic floor muscles contract at 0.8 seconds intervals for 5 to 12 times in females and 3 to 6 times in males.

A sexual response cycle that is associated with high sexual tension but no orgasm can lead to a prolonged resolution phase. There are no reliable data on the effects of hastened sexual response cycle induced by masturbation and its effect on the functionality of a cycle induced by sex with a partner. The woman' response to masturbation may be rapid and may hasten her response to foreplay, leading to orgasm prior to copulation.

The *resolution phase* involves return of the body into its pre-excitement phase. Blood pressure and heart rate fall initially below normal levels and return to normal levels soon thereafter. The body muscles relax; with generalised sweat, more marked in the palms and soles. The generalised vaso-dilatation helps to drain blood and decrease pelvic engorgement. It leads to gradual loss of erection in males, with some degree of residual engorgement, which is higher at younger age. In females, the clitoris returns to its pre-arousal position, the labia returns to its normal size and position and the vagina relaxes. The breasts and areola decrease in size and the nipples lose their erection. In men, the scrotum relaxes and the testes descend. The resolution phase in men varies between individuals and at different stages of life, being shorter in younger age.

The *refractory phase* is the period that follows the orgasmic phase in men, and during which a second erection can not be achieved. It may range from 5 minutes to 24 hours or more. There is no refractory period for the majority of women, which allows the woman to return to an excitation phase followed by orgasm. This what Chinese early writings described as limitless *Yin* in woman.

The sense of relaxation that accompanies loss of muscle tension, promotes personal experience between the couple and lead to a sense of closeness and intimacy. A person shutting himself from his/her partner, during this phase, may precipitate the wrong perception of rejection.

Women are capable of multiple orgasms, moving from one orgasm into a plateau phase, followed by another orgasm. Men must undergo the resolution phase first before being able to achieve another orgasm. Some women do not achieve orgasm but experience compassionate, loving relationship and intimacy with their partners. It is questionable whether therapy is required in such cases. There is a danger of mediatisation of what otherwise could be a variant of normal; but the therapist is bound by a duty of care to respond to client's complaints of lack of orgasm.

Intimacy transforms the sex act into love making experience. Intimacy could be sub-divided into physical and emotional intimacy; with one perpetuating the other in a vicious circle. It is an essential goal of many human relationships leading into sexual intercourse. It is a catalyst of the physical relationship and makes human sexuality emotionally fulfilling. It encompasses commitment, adjustment, concern, endurance of relationship and sense of belonging to each other.

Physical sexual relationships, without intimacy, carry the risk of predictability, dissatisfaction and possibly looking for sexual gratification elsewhere. The initial courtship experience gives the couple the opportunity of mutual sexual discovery and learning about each others' erotic interests. Circumventing this stage of sexual relationship caries risk of losing interest and satisfaction. Courtship forms the basis of the sensate focus exercise; where the couple re-learn about sharing the act of giving and receiving pleasure, without the pressures of sexual intercourse.

Part II: Sexual Dysfunctions

Chapter III

Puberty, Sex
and Sexual Dysfunctions

Puberty is the period during which boys and girls attaining adult secondly sexual characters and reproductive capacity. The age of puberty, in both boys and girls has declined with improvements in living standards, nutrition and health; contrary to the age of menopause which seem to be fixed. The precise mechanism controlling the onset of puberty is still obscure. The onset of puberty is associated with a combination of decreased hypothalamic sensitivity to the negative feedback and increased gonadal sensitivity; suggesting a dual maturation process in both organs. The Gonadotrophine Releasing Hormone (GnRH)neurones that developed in the nasal placode, migrates to the hypothalamus. Pulsatile secretion of GnRH leads to pituitary stimulation and pulsatile secretion gonadotrophins, namely, Follicle Stimulating Hormone (FSH) and Luteinising Hormone (LH); and consequently gonadal steroids. The pubertal growth spurt is controlled by a surge in Growth Hormone (GH) and Insulin-like Growth Factor 1 (IGF-1).

In males, testosterone production starts to increase from the bone age of 12 and continuing with a steep rise up to the age of 15 to 17. It reaches adult levels by early to mid-twenties, when the testicles provides 95% whilst the adrenal glands 5%. There is an initial surge of LH and FSH at puberty but a decline later, due to the negative feedback from the increased testosterone levels. Male earliest physical changes appear in the growth of the testes and scrotum, around the age of 11; followed by appearance of pubic hair. Penile growth appears a year later. The first ejaculation occurs a year after penile growth. The body growth spurt starts between 10.5 and 16 years and is associated with deepening of voice. One in three boys may notice breast enlargement which recedes after a year.

Androgen increase during puberty is responsible for the penile, scrotal and testicular enlargement and sensitivity to tactile stimulation. Androgens are also responsible for the masculine body hair pattern, voice deepening, sweat and sebaceous gland activation, bone growth, increased muscle bulk and epiphysis closure. Testosterone is essential for spermatogenesis, prostatic and seminal vesicles secretions.

Puberty in the females starts between the ages of 9 and 13 years; with breast development and growth of public hair. Breast enlargement is associated with fluctuation in oestrogens levels. Menarche occurs between 11.5 and 15.5 years. The mean age of menarche has declined during the last century. Initially there are some anovulatory cycles; then the well established ovulatory cycles ensue; when oestrogens reach a high enough level. The growth spurt starts and ends earlier than in boys.

Oestrogens are essential for the normal pubertal development of the uterus, fallopian tubes, vagina, vulva and skeletal growth. They are responsible for breast enlargement in pubertal girls. They indirectly stimulate ovulation and endometrial proliferation. In males, oestrogens may be responsible for puberty associated gynaecomastia, bone growth and epiphysis closure.

Progestagens change the oestrogen induced proliferative endometrium into a secrertory one. They maintain pregnancy and promote the growth of breast alveoli that lead to milk production. They have some androgenic effects. There could be some role of androgens in the female normal pubertal developments, namely body hair, sebaceous glands, labiae majorae, clitoris and epiphysis closure.

Clinical Significance

Young women and men may go through a period of partnership exploration. This may lead to multiplicity of partnerships, unplanned or unprotected sexual intercourse and consequently sexually transmitted infections (STIs). Underage sex should be handled with due care and better understanding of the local, country, state laws and regulations. The clinician need to discuss the risks of STIs with the young person respectfully, openly and sympathetically; to give her/him the opportunity to make an informed decision about having tests to rule out STIs.

There is a growing understanding that dedicated "young person's clinics" that deal with issues affecting teenagers; like family planning, STIs and sexual health, are best served by staff that have the expertise and willingness to care for this age cohort. Teenagers presenting for "sexual health advice" should be handled with a professional sense of duty of care. The Clinician's own morality should not override his/her own professional responsibility to provide an objective clinical assessment, investigations and treatment.

The discovery of hymeneal remnants may cause anxiety and alarm to the couple. The problem could simply be resolved by assurance. Excision under local anaesthesia, is rarely required. In young men, frenular tears pose a more challenging problem; as their repair is associated with fibrosis and the consequent vulnerability to future tears. Wearing a condom provide a degree of protection to the vulnerable fraenulum. A sensitive young male, or his parents, may express concern with pubertal gynaecomastia. The explanation of the temporary nature of the condition and its cause provides enough for assurance.

Premature ejaculation is a common presentation of sexual dysfunction in young men. It could be resolved in most circumstances by natural methods (e.g. wearing a thick condom, penile glans and/or penile base squeeze) or with pharmaco-therapy (e.g. Selective Serotonin Reuptake Inhibitors), on the basis of sporadic and as required regimen.

Vulvodynia, in teenagers, is most likely caused by an organic condition. Essential Vulvodynia does occur in young women and requires a sympathetic clinical approach. Dyspareunia requires through assessment and investigations. Undiagnosed PID may compromise the young woman's future fertility, in addition to pelvic pain and risk of ectopic pregnancy. The association between sub-acute pelvic inflammatory disease (PID) and dyspareunia, should be taken seriously. The clinician should follow a systematic approach of differential diagnosis, aiming to proactively exclude PID in any young woman presenting with dyspareunia.

Hypogonadism and Delayed Puberty

The clinical features of male hypogonadism depend on the stage of onset. Androgen deficiency during foetal development results in *genital ambiguity*. The failure of Leydig Cells and androgen deficiency before puberty lead to *Eunuchoidism*. The features of eunuchoidism include skeletal disproportion.

The upper to lower body ratio is less than 1. The arm span is more than 2 inches greater than the height. The pre-adolescent male hair distribution and infantile genitalia persist. There is usually poor development of muscle mass. Understandably, these conditions are likely to be seen by various specialists (e.g. Endocrinologists and Paediatricians). *Primary hypo-gonadism* may present with delayed puberty. If puberty is established, regression of the male secondary sexual characteristics requires a very long period to be notable. A young man's complaint of decreased libido, poor erection, loss of pubic and axillary hair, the development of gynaecomastia and/or hot flushes should arouse clinical suspicion. Causes of testicular damage should be considered, namely: Cryptorchidism, post pubertal testicular inflammation, torsion, or excessive exposure to heat and/or radiotherapy. Chronic disease, chronic alcoholism and chronic intake of illicit drugs can have a negative effect on spermatogenesis and testosterone production; either by direct primary effect on the testicles or secondary to disturbance in the gonadal-pituitary-hypothalamic axis. Cancer chemotherapy reduces spermatogenesis, in a dose related relationship. It may also compromise the Testosterone production by direct affect on the Leydig cells. The association of loss of libido with headache, visual disturbances, gynaecomastia and galactorrhoea should direct the attention and investigations for pituitary tumour.

The spontaneous diurnal and nocturnal erections are androgen dependent and markedly compromised in hypo-gonadal patients; but restored with Testosterone Replacement Therapy (TRT). It is possible that there are 2 separate central processes; one that leads to spontaneous erection and is androgen dependent, whilst the other is relating to erection in response to erotic stimuli, which remains intact in cases of androgen deficiency. Hypo-gonadal men, receiving TRT, report return of libido, restoration of ejaculation and elevation of mood.

Delayed breast development in a 14 years old girl prompts assessment. Excessive exercise, obesity, malnutrition or emotional deprivation can delay growth development and should be excluded before extensive investigations. Systemic and chronic diseases are associated with delayed growth (e.g. cystic fibrosis, asthma, rheumatoid arthritis, inflammatory bowel disease, …). Endocrinopathies (e.g. Diabetes, hypo and hyper thyroidism, growth hormone deficiency,….) may also present as delayed puberty. The association of pituitary hormone deficiency with headache and/ or visual disturbances should direct the clinician to exclude pituitary tumours. Chromosomal conditions (e.g.Turner and Down Syndromes) and gonadotrophic hypo and hyperactivity are the remit of sub-specialised care.

Chapter IV

Ageing, Sex and Sexual Dysfunctions

The progressive improvements of living standards, medical care and education reduced the impact of human disease and improved longevity. The longer life expectancy, for women, lead to a higher number of women than men in the later age groups. There is a shared understanding between the public and the medical profession that sexual activity declines in both men and women with age. Clinicians also appreciate that the aging couple continue to have sexual relationships and need assistance at different stages of their life, for different reasons. New partnerships have also their own expectations; as separation and new relationships are becoming part of society's norms. The improved quality of life for aging men and women, better management of what otherwise could have been disabling conditions (e.g. Menopause) and the readily available new treatments (e.g. Phoshpo-diesterase type 5 inhibitors) improved the prospects of better sexual relationships, for older people. Population studies and surveys continue to be the principle source of evidence and add to the body of clinical experience. Understanding the natural age related changes, their causes and implications, should help the clinician and the couple to proactively manage changes in sexual function and to treat dysfunctions. A well-adjusted couple would learn how to adapt to each others physiological changes. The clinician could help to promote inter-personal adjustment; and provide treatment when required. Simple measures (e.g. phospho-diesterase type 5 inhibitors for impotence or vaginal oestrogens for atrophic vaginitis) may be all that is needed.

The Effects of Aging on Libido

Sexual desire, in both women and men, declines gradually with progressing age. Adolescent males experience increased sexual desire in parallel with testosterone secretion, leading to progressive interest in the opposite sex. The progressive increase in testosterone levels is paralleled with increased libido; reaching its peak in adulthood. Middle aged men experience gradual change in sexual desire. Aging men continue to report sexual desire. In older men, health, social, economic and relationship factors play a complex role. The number of men reporting "loss of libido" increases progressively with each decade of age groups. The role of testosterone at this stage is not entirely clear. Testosterone role in older men is evident, when levels are lower than the generally accepted range of normal; which provides the basis for Testosterone Replacement Therapy (TRT).

Sexual desire in women is more difficult to explore; due to lack of studies, especially in the earlier age groups (i.e. during adolescence and adulthood). Observational studies indicate a clear interest of adolescent girls in the opposite sex. The role of oestrogens in developing the reproductive tract, genital organs and secondary sexual characteristics is well established. Oestrogens spurt during puberty is associated with expressed female interest in the opposite sex, which suggests a correlation. Analysis of the correlation between female sex hormones and sexual desire is challenged by their cyclical pattern. Studies indicate a decline in female sexual desire from the middle age onwards; with dramatic decline after the menopause. There is persistent and gradual decline in sexual desire, evidenced by the increasing percentage of women reporting loss of libido in each decade of age groups. For each age group, women reporting "loss of desire" to sex were higher than their male counterparts. There is no clear hormonal correlation.

The prevalence figures of low sexual desire between men and women suggest that the condition is more pronounced in females. Studies indicate that females' report, distress with sexual dysfunction, more in the pre-menopausal and post-menopausal group, accounting for 15% of cases, as compared with 10% of younger and middle aged women. Patients' studies suggest the prevalence of reduced desire in younger women is generally in the region of 1 in 10; but 1 in 20 only make complains.

Post menopausal oestrogens deficiency is the most common hormonal disorder contributing into sexual dysfunction. Vulvo-vaginal atrophy, vaginal dryness, post menopausal Vulvo-vaginitis, loss of vaginal wall elasticity and stenosis are single or combined causes, which may lead to Vulvodynia and Dyspareunia; and considerably reduce the desire for sex. Pre-existing emotional conditions do influence the outcome of therapy. Women who have had "hysterectomy and bilateral oophorectomy" for a benign disease, report improved sexual desire with the consequent hormone replacement therapy. On the contrary, pre-existing depression or loss of libido, make the woman particularly vulnerable to sexual dysfunction, post hysterectomy and oohporectomy.

The Affects of Aging on Sexual Response

The sexual response is mostly vasculo-genic response, which requires the integrity of neuro-genic mechanisms and balanced hormonal factors. Decrease in tactile sensitivity, with advancing age, could also be perpetuated by chronic disease (e.g. Diabetes Mellitus). Consequently, in older men, erections require longer and more direct tactile stimulation; with decreasing effect of psychic stimulation. Early morning erections and nocturnal erections also decline. The ability to sustain erections becomes shorter; with continued loss of penile rigidity. Eventually erections are not adequate for vaginal penetration. Seminal expulsive force declines gradually due to loss of pelvic floor muscle tone; leading patients to complain of "seeping and dribbling of semen rather than spurting out". The total volume of seminal discharge per orgasm declines, due to the aging process in the testes, prostate and Cowper's glands. The previously experienced adolescent desire, to reach climax following sexual stimulation, declines progressively. The reduced ejaculatory demand enables the aging male to continue foreplay without the pressures of desire to reach a climax. An aging male's spouse may erroneously have the impression that he does not wish to proceed to intercourse and she is "no longer desirable". On the contrary, extended foreplay, due to decreased ejaculatory demand, can promote satisfaction of the aging male's partner. The refractory period extends gradually from a few minutes in early adolescent hood, to a day in middle life and a week in later age. It is a major contributing factor in the decline of intercourse frequency.

In aging women, drug industry sponsorship biased research towards menopause; leading to less data regarding the earlier age groups. The effect of natural menopause is not universal to all women. Many women do not complain of sexual dysfunctions following menopause; and some of the complaints (e.g. loss of libido) may not respond fully to oestrogen replacement. Vaginal dryness, vulvo-vaginal atrophy and bladder base inflammation (i.e. Trigonitis) are usually expressed in dyspareunia. The ensuing pain is bound to lead to apprehension, anxiety, sympathetic autonomic overdrive and consequent reduction in pelvic congestion and exaggerated dryness. Post menopausal oestrogens deprivation leads to vulvo-vaginal atrophy. Its severe form may be associated with "atrophic vaginitis". Lack of intercourse and disuse of the vagina, combined with the gradual loss of tissue elasticity, and may lead to vaginal narrowing. The woman's fears of pain have a negative influence on her desire for sex. The aging woman complains of decline in vaginal lubrication; as a separate problem or in combination with the above conditions. This is not entirely explainable by the post-menopausal decline in oestrogens. The decline in vaginal lubrication continues well beyond the menopause; affecting half of the women in their 50s and up to three-quarters in their 70s. Some younger women complain of dryness after having children and/or taking higher progesterone containing contraception pills. Studies suggest that the frequency of orgasm, in women, does not decline much with age; but the resolution phase becomes more rapid. Sexual arousal and orgasmic disorders are reported less frequently by women, than men. Age related Gynaecological conditions (e.g. pelvic floor deficiency and prolepses) contribute to sexual dysfunction and benefit from reconstructive surgery and/or physiotherapy.

Hormone Replacement Therapy (HRT) and Female Sexuality

The female menopause is associated with resistance of the ovarian follicles to Gonadotrophine stimulation. The process is gradual and progressive, up to a point of complete cessation of ovarian activity, dramatic decline in the ovarian production of oestrogens and consequently menstruation. It starts gradually, some 10 years prior to menopause, which is currently fixed around the average age of 50 in industrialised countries. Contrary to menarche, the age at which menopause arrives did not change with improvements in living, health and nutritional standards. The serum levels of follicle stimulating hormone (FSH) and luteinizing hormone (LH) increase, due to lack of ovarian steroids' negative feedback. A 10-15 folds rise in FSH and 3 folds rise in LH are diagnostic of menopause. The levels provide an objective confirmation of early menopause. Early menopause may be iatrogenic and follow pelvic radiotherapy, some cancer chemotherapy and or oophorectomy. Familial early menopause could be found in women with no clear underlying aetiology (i.e. Premature Menopause). Oestradiol secretion from the post-menopausal ovary ceases; but some degree of conversion of steroids into Oestradiol continues in the peripheral tissues, mainly fat. Testosterone and androstenedione continue to be produced by the ovarian stroma; in addition to androgens from the adrenal glands.

Menopausal hot flushes, insomnia, emotional changes, urinary tract symptoms, dyspareunia and/or osteoporosis, will influence the woman's over-all sense of well being and interest in sexual activity. The improvement of these issues, with Hormone replacement Therapy (HRT), will have an indirect impact on sexual activity. On the contrary, the effect of oestrogens replacement therapy on the woman's libido is not as evident as that of testosterone therapy.

Sexual desire, arousal and sexual fantasies are related to androgen replacement but not oestrogens therapy. Androgen-oestrogens combination improves sexual desire, sexual arousal and number of fantasises; an effect which is not achieved either by placebo or Oestradiol alone. Neither oestrogen nor testosterone therapy have a proven direct effect on coital or orgasmic frequency. Oestrogens would have an indirect effect, through the alleviation of vulvo vaginal atrophy, vaginal dryness, atrophic vulvo-vaginitis, bladder base symptoms and/or dyspareunia.

The wide varieties of HRT preparations provide patients with a range of choice; namely: skin patches, gels, nasal sprays, tablets and implants. The aim of HRT is to deliver a set dosage of Oestrogens into the blood stream with added Progesterone to reduce the risk of uterine cancer.

Alternatively, the patient may elect to have hysterectomy or insertion of progesterone containing Intra-Uterine Device (e.g. Mirena). Cyclical combined HRT preparations provide 14 days of progesterone; in either the monthly or three monthly cyclical HRT. The later have the convenience of reduced frequency of vaginal bleeding (i.e. once every three months).

Continuous combined HRT preparation is more suitable for post-menopausal women, who ceased to have a period for a year or more; or women after the age of 54 and who had been on cyclical preparations before.

Topical vaginal preparations (i.e. vaginal oestrogens cream or pessaries) are beneficial for patients who complain of genital symptoms (e.g. vulvo-vaginal atrophy, atrophic vaginitis…) and have reservations about systemic

HRT. Some patients who are already using systemic HRT may require additional supportive vaginal application. It is important that the clinician gives the patient the opportunity to make an informed decision. HRT is associated with reduced risk of osteoporosis and developing colorectal cancer. This should be balanced against the slight increased risk of venous thrombo-embolism, and/or breast cancer. These balances fall outside the scope of this text.

Testosterone Replacement Therapy (TRT) for Men

Age associated Testosterone Deficiency Syndrome (TDS) is also known as *Late Onset Hypogonadism (LOH)* and affects some men in advancing age. The diagnosis is reached by the clinical picture and low testosterone levels. The prevalence of LOH varies between different studies; depending on the demographics of the referred and studied population. It is thought to affect some 2-4% of men above the age of 50. The symptoms of LOH include: loss of concentration, reduced wellbeing, fatigue, depression, reduced muscle mass, reduced body hair, hot flushes and sweats. Reduced libido, decreased morning erections, reduced penile sensitivity; inability to obtain and/or maintain erection, ejaculatory dysfunction could also be blamed, in part, on reduced testosterone levels.

Testosterone Replacement Therapy (TRT) leads to reversion in several of these symptoms; which suggest that functional testosterone deficiency is the main underlying cause of LOH. There are risk factors underlying LOH. They include chronic diseases conditions (e.g. diabetes mellitus, arthritis, chronic obstructive airway disease and HIV). Obesity, metabolic syndrome, excessive alcohol intake are contributing factors for LOH and represent areas where there is a place for preventive treatment. Iatrogenic factors of LOH include longstanding opiate therapy and treatment for prostatic cancer (i.e. Androgen Deprivation Therapy).

The LOH condition is usually discovered during the course of investigations for erectile dysfunction and/or reduced libido. None of the symptoms is specific to a low androgen state but should raise suspicion about its possible deficiency; which should prompt Testosterone early morning measurement. Testosterone levels may be transiently reduced (e.g. acute illness); therefore repeated tests, on more than one occasion, are required. There is no general agreement on the lower limit of the normal.

There is widespread agreement that a level above 12 nmol/l (350 mg/dl) does not require replacement. Levels below 8 nmol/l (230 mg/dl) would usually benefit from testosterone replacement.

Luteinising hormone (LH), Prolactin and Sex Hormone Binding Globulin (SHBG) should be part of the overall investigation. LH levels will assist in differentiating between primary and secondary Hypogonadism. A high prolactin level would lead to a remarkable reduction in testosterone level.

Late onset Hypogonadism is an indication for testosterone replacement therapy (TRT). Patients who had breast or prostatic cancers have a clear contraindication for TRT. Severe congestive heart failure, obstructive sleep apnoea and significant erythrocytosis are relative contraindications and require high degree of caution and balance of pros and cons of TRT. Natural testosterone preparations (transdermal, subdermal, intramuscular, buccal or oral) are effective.

It is wise to start with a short acting preparation first; to assess the response and side effects. Obese men are more likely to report adverse effects. TRT restores and/or enhances responsiveness to PDE-5 Inhibitors, most notably in diabetic patients.

The long-term sequellae of testosterone replacement therapy are not yet known; therefore, we should exercise caution. If the patient decides on TRT, the clinician should assess the patient for prostatic cancer; throughout therapy. Digital examination and Prostatic Specific Antigen (PSA) should be part of the initial assessment and PSA should be measured at 3, 6 and 12 months initially and annually thereafter. PSA increments of more than 1.4 ng/ml warrant investigation for prostatic cancer.

The clinician should ascertain therapeutic testosterone levels of 15 nmol/l and monitor total and free testosterone levels, SHBG and albumin, throughout the treatment program. There should be a measureable benefit to the patient from therapy, evidenced by improvement in signs and symptoms of testosterone deficiency (i.e. improved libido, sexual and muscle functions). If there is no improvement after several months, the treatment should be discontinued and the patient counselled for the further management of his presenting condition.

Ingestible preparations are more likely to cause erythrocytosis and therefore regular follow-ups with full blood counts are necessary. Dose re-adjustment, to keep the haematocrit value below 50%, should be attempted first; otherwise venesection may be necessary.

Testosterone Replacement Therapy (TRT) for Women

The role of androgens in women is not clear; due to the scarcity of scientific research. Steroid hormones receptors are intra-cellular and influenced by other hormonal factors; including other steroidal hormones. The levels and functionality of the steroid hormones intra-cellular receptors play an important role in the eventual effects of steroidal hormones. Therefore, the mere assessment of the serum hormone levels does not necessarily correspond to physiological, pathological or pharmacological changes.

The ovaries provide 50% of female Testosterone whilst the adrenal glands provide the other 50% It is notable that androgen levels decline gradually in women after their mid-30s; who may lose up to 2/3 of their adrenal source. Ovarian androgen production continues to decline, gradually and persistently, up to and following menopause. Bilateral oophorectomy leads to loss of ovarian androgen production and precursors, which reduces the overall peripheral conversion. The capacity of testosterone to bind to plasma albumin and globulin (Steroid Hormone Binding Globulin: SHBG), and the readiness of these plasma proteins to vary their serum levels, in response to other plasma steroids, contributes to the difficulty in drawing practical levels for clinical assessment. SHBG levels can vary with exogenous oestrogens (e.g. contraceptive pills), hyper or hypo-thyroidism, obesity and aging. SHBG level fluctuates and consequently affects the testosterone levels. Oestrogens, hyper-thyroidism and/or women of increasing age have increased levels of SHBG and therefore testosterone. Obesity and hypo-thyroidism reduce the SHBG levels and consequently lead to lower testosterone levels.

Hormonal assays for a woman with sexual dysfunction are indicated to exclude diabetes, thyroid disease and/or premature menopause. Thyroid function tests, prolactin, LH, FSH and/or SHBG levels are indicated, according to the woman's presentation. There is no practical or clinical case for requesting testosterone levels for women, as part of TRT.

The role of testosterone therapy in women complaining of sexual dysfunction should be considered as part of the general management of the individual woman's case. It is generally considered that women with SHBG levels above 160 nmol/L do not require testosterone therapy. Topical gels or creams or transdermal patches circumvent the first-pass hepatic metabolism effect which is well known in oral therapy. Topical preparations are suitable for women who are not undergoing operative procedures There was a time when Gynaecologists used testosterone in addition to oestrogen implants, for post-oophorectomy women, to maintain their sexual desire. The patient requires explicit counselling regarding the side-effects of androgen, especially hirsutism and acne. The overt nature of hirsutism and acne can make them more distressing to the patient than the covert sexual dysfunction; therefore, require an informed consent prior to the initiation of therapy. Patients usually present with multiple symptoms and a mixed picture. A woman who is experiencing pain during intercourse is likely to become apprehensive and fearful of the recurrence of pain and lose desire, arousability and the ability to reach orgasm. Therefore, it is important to identify the precipitating cause, as the first step in reversing other elements of the cycle. The clinician should consider the effect of some drugs on sexual functions (e.g. anti-hypertensives, anti-psychotics, anti-depressants); which may benefit from a simple change of prescribing. The long term effects of testosterone therapy for women are not well researched; therefore its use is best reserved to patients undergoing pre-menopausal oophorectomy. Data on long term use and breast safety is lacking.

Short acting preparations provide the opportunity and advantage of assessment of the benefits and side effects; which allows for treatment withdrawal if the patient finds the side effects distressing. There must be a measurable benefit to the patient, to justify the continuation of treatment. If the patient is planning to continue on a long-term therapy, she should have follow up measurements of her blood glucose levels and lipid profile. Patients with diabetes and/or hyper-lipidaemia should benefit from nutritional counselling. They would require measurement of fasting lipids and glucose levels, after 6 months of treatment. If abnormal levels continued, despite changes in the patients' lifestyle or intake of lipid lowering drugs, there is a case for cessation of testosterone therapy.

Chapter V

Classification of Sexual Dysfunctions

Sexual Dysfunctions

1. Sexual Desire Disorders

- Female / male   hypoactive sexual desire disorder
- Female / male   hyperactive sexual desire disorder
- Female / male   sexual aversion disorders
- Female / male   sexual phobias

2. Sexual Arousal Disorders

- Male: Erectile dysfunction
- Female: Lack of vaginal lubrication

3. Orgasmic Disorders

- Male Premature Ejaculation
  - Delayed Ejaculation
  - Retrograde Ejaculation

- – Painful Ejaculation
- Female Delayed/Retarded Orgasm
    - – Anorgasmia

4. Sexual Dissatisfaction

Sexual dysfunction could be classified into sexual desire; arousal, orgasmic and/or sexual pain disorders. Each of the categories is sub-divided into: *primary*, when the condition is life long and existing since coitarche; versus *secondary*, when there is a problem free interval. Each sub-category is either *generalised*, when it happen globally and irrespective of the partner, versus *situational*, when it is relating to a particular situation or partner. Each condition is graded as *mild, moderate or severe*, according to its impact on the patient and/or partners life. For each category, the underlying aetiology could be *psychogenic, organic, mixed or unknown*.

Patients, usually, present with multiple symptoms and mixed pictures. A woman who is experiencing pain during intercourse is likely to become apprehensive and fearful of the recurrence of pain; lose her desire, arousability and/or ability to reach orgasm. A male who is unable to obtain or maintain an erection will become apprehensive and lose desire; in a vicious circle. Therefore, it is important to identify the principal and main precipitating cause of the sexual dysfunction, to be able to reveres the disrupted elements of the sexual response cycle.

Sexual dissatisfaction, defined as discontent and/or lack of enjoyment in the sexual relationship, may or may not be associated with sexual dysfunctions. There is a strong association between sexual dissatisfaction and "sexual difficulties". It is likely that some sexual dysfunctions are tolerated by some couples, who otherwise enjoy a happy interpersonal relationship. It is self evident that individuals who present to the sexual dysfunction clinic are dissatisfied with their sexual relationship. Inter-personal conflicts, difficulty in relaxation, unsatisfactory foreplay and/or lack of enjoyment, are some examples that would lead to sexual dissatisfaction.

Chapter VI

Erectile Dysfunction (ED)

Prevalence

Erectile Dysfunction (ED) encapsulates patient's complaints of persistent or recurrent in-ability to attain and/or maintain an erection that is sufficient to permit satisfactory sexual intercourse. The wide medical community recognises the significance of the complaint and its impact on the quality of life of the incumbent patient and his partner. ED has worldwide significance due to improving health standards, increasing survival and the high prevalence of ED. There are records in history of the recognition of ED and the treatment attempts with prosthesis, concoctions and remedies. Several national studies have calculated the percentage prevalence and number of annual new cases per 1000 men, who suffered ED. There are differences of prevalence between studies; due to age group, social, demographic factors and study design methodology. An American study identified 52% of men aged 40-70 years to complain of ED; 1 in 10 of whom complained of complete ED and 1 in 4 moderate Ed. Analysis of the results estimated that 26 new cases per 1000 men develop ED annually. The prevalence increases with age progression, from 20% in the fifth decade, to 30% and 40% in the sixth and seventh decades. The observation that 1 in 2-3 men with ED have an underlying organic cause should prompt a clinical exclusion process. One in four ED patients have a cardiovascular and/or urinary co-morbidity; whilst one in six is diabetic and one in ten has neurological condition. Endocrine conditions are rare but are amenable to treatment. Erectile dysfunction may be the earliest symptom of these underlying organic causes. The ease with which men may obtain oral therapy for ED could lead to the late diagnosis of underlying organic conditions that may otherwise benefit from early diagnosis and treatment.

Aetiology

Erection is a vascular mechanism that involves a fine balance between penile arterial dilatation, cavernous trabecular smooth muscle relaxation and corporeal veno-occlusion; and is controlled by neural and hormonal factors. Any condition that damage any or all of these factors can lead to ED.

Cardio-vascular diseases share common risk factors with ED, namely obesity, lack of exercise, smoking, hyper-cholesterolaemia and metabolic syndrome. ED may be the earliest indication of cardiovascular disease. One in four men suffering ED has evidence of cardiovascular disease. Coronary artery disease and peripheral arterial occlusion may be discovered first during ED investigations. Studies have shown that men who undertook exercise in mid-life had 70% less risk for ED, in comparison to those who did not. Another study of lifestyle intervention identified correlation between Body Mass Index (BMI), Erectile Dysfunction and physical activity. It would be prudent to consider a risk reduction strategy.

Diabetes mellitus is one of the most common causes of ED, influenced by type, duration and metabolic compensation. The majority of diabetic patients are diagnosed well before the ED; but some are diagnosed first during the course of ED investigations. Diabetes related autonomic neuropathy and impairment of the vascular mechanisms are the main aetiological causes of ED. Associated athero-sclerotic changes in the iliac, pudendal and penile arteries; perpetuated by penile capillary dysfunction lead to ED. Somatic, para-sympathetic and sympathetic neuropathy reduce both afferent and efferent stimuli and consequently erection, emission and ejaculation. The synthesis and release of neurotransmitters are dysfunctional (e.g. NO, VIP, ILGF, …). The cavernous tissue show reduced smooth muscle mass and increased collagen and fibrous tissue. Metabolic syndrome and Hyper-lipidaemia, which usually take place in association with diabetes mellitus, can lead to or perpetuate ED. The vasculo-genic effect of atheromatous changes, narrowing of medium and small sized vessels and consequent deficient peripheral circulations underline ED aetiology. Consequently, the patient usually suffers from other associated cardio-vascular and hypertensive disorders. Each can cause ED on its own, in association with other disease conditions and their drug therapies. A typical compounded situation is a patient with diabetes mellitus, hyper-lipidaemia, hypertension, who smokes and drinks heavily and undertaking anti-hypertensive and anti-lipidaemic therapy.

Lower urinary tract symptoms (LUTS) are prominent in one of four ED patients. The medical and/or surgical management of these symptoms are associated with ED.

Drug induced ED ranks high on the list of organic aetiology. All anti-hypertensive agents can lead to ED; but most notoriously diuretics and beta-blockers. Anti-depressants and anti-psychotics on their own are associated with ED to variable degrees. The underlying clinical indication for these drugs is usually a cause of ED; which is then perpetuated by the drug therapy. Regular and heavy use of recreational drugs (e.g. marijuana, heroin, cocaine and methadone) leads to ED. The addiction patients' drug associated health and social problems usually take priority over ED. The chronic intake of anti-histamenics is not a common cause of ED in clinical practice; but drugs in this group can potentially lead to ED. Anti-androgens prescribing should be the territory of sub-specialised care, with clear instructions on side-effects and ED.

Alcohol is a challenging drug to evaluate in clinical practice. Its effect varies with dosage, age, habituation, sex and race. Men from East Asian background are more vulnerable to the effects of alcohol. The history of alcohol intake is often underestimated by the male patient. Its effects on the individual are also variable. In small dosages, it could produce a state of relaxation. Excessive intake and/or responsiveness can lead to impotence. The male partner's loss of time orientation, in response to alcohol, may lead to him to the false impression of better sexual performance. The input of the female partner, into the clinical assessment, brings another dimension into the case history. The influence of the expectation from alcohol intake is significant and at times is more important than the pharmacological effects. In clinical trials, patients who believed that they are under the effect of alcohol, following the intake of a look-alike and taste-alike beverage, responded in a lucid manner to pornographic stimuli. Those who were told that the drink was alcoholic; but in fact was look-alike and taste-alike, but not alcoholic, subconsciously suppressed their sexual responses to the pornographic stimuli. The effect is more of expectancy than pharmacological. *Life style factors* are one of the most common causes of ED in clinical practice. The combination of a process of aging, change in employment or social circumstances, interpersonal relationship difficulties and the anxiety associated with any or all of these factors can lead to ED. The typical scenario is a late middle-aged man who does not draw satisfaction or quality of life from his own job, feels threatened and either suffered or afraid of suffering a relationship failure. The compounding sense of anxiety, insecurity and apprehension culminate to ED. Alcoholism, precipitated or perpetuated by any of these factors, will contribute to ED. The man's experience of an episode of ED leads to anxiety; and the cycle goes on.

Neuro-genic conditions are usually complex and well expressed clinically in many other stigmata, before the diagnosis of ED. Presentation with neurogenic ED is usually part of the clinical picture. Parkinson's Disease, Multiple Sclerosis and Stroke are common causes of ED. The patient care pathway of these conditions should proactively include the management of ED. The clinician should not await the patient and/or partner to complain of ED. Inter-Vertebral Disc disease as a cause of ED, is a worthwhile diagnosis, where there are benefits in early treatment. Spinal cord disorders are complex and require the expertise of specialised and multidisciplinary Neuro-Surgical team. ED is part of some neuro-genic conditions, when the general condition and care requirements subsume the ED problem (e.g. Dementia). Uraemic polyneuropathy is becoming a less common cause due to improved care for kidney failure.

Pelvic, lower abdominal and/or retro-peritoneal major surgery or radiotherapy are associated with damage to peripheral nerves and/or medium and small sized vessels leading to a compounded effect of neuro--vascular ED. The improved survival of these procedures should be matched with improved quality of life, including early rehabilitation and proactive management of ED.

Endocrine disorders are rare causes but benefit from early diagnosis. There treatment may rectify the underlying ED. Hypo-gonadism, hypo-and hyper-thyroidism, hyper-prolactinaemia and Cushing's disease are relatively rare causes of ED. A hormonal profile at the outset of the assessment for ED should be part of the work up, to exclude these conditions that are rare but worthwhile diagnosing.

Cavernous tissue dysfunction is part of the aging process leading to ED. Cavernous damage due to fibrosis may follow Priapism or penile fracture.

The Clinical Assessment of Erectile Dysfunction

The clinical setting and atmosphere for assessing couples with sexual dysfunction should benefit from a relaxed and sympathetic approach. Many patients do not complain of their condition due to embarrassment or past experience with unsympathetic response of medical practitioners. The self diagnosis of Sexual Dysfunction in a relationship is usually reliable in most cases. In some relationships, it takes the expertise of an independent practitioner to identify the partner/s misperceptions, compounded feeling of guilt and/or defensive blame. Meeting the couple together, at some stage of the clinical consultation, is valuable. It helps to identify any dynamics of tensions between the partners; and can help to direct the management.

History of past relationships is helpful in identifying whether the ED is situational and partner related or generalised due to lack of desire or arousability. This part of the history is better achieved during one-to-one consultation. It is equally important to meet each partner separately, as s/he may express concern that s/he perceive to be embarrassing to the other partner. At times, either partner is open for discussion only when the other is absent. The prospective of the problem may be different between partners. It is important to determine the individual patient's own perception and assessment of his own condition, as with that of his other partner. Dual self-administered questionnaires, for both patient and partner, completed separately before the consultation, will highlight areas of differences in perception between the couple.

Disharmony between the partners' sexual response cycle is a cause for problems, on its own, or combined with other ED causes. A common example is lack of synchronization in reaching the excitation phase. The speed with which the male can reach full erection and readiness for penetration may not correspond with the woman's progress with excitation and vaginal lubrication. Attempted intercourse at this point may lead to difficulty in penetration. Undue stretching of the dry vulva may lead to skin cracks and Dyspareunia. This may lead to apprehension, fear and/or Vaginismus. The clinician should facilitate better understanding between the partners; to bring harmonious and synchronous sexual response cycle.

The availability of oral therapy for ED has changed the referral pattern to specialised ED units. Current examples of referrals include patients with complicated medical history, multiple drug therapy and/or failure or side-effects to ongoing oral ED therapy. There are also secondary referrals of patients who have experienced decline of response to their ED oral therapy, after the initial years of response to treatment.

Past and current medical history should be available for consultations for sexual dysfunction. Some of the long term medications contribute to ED, whilst alternatives may be better suited. The co-operation of the medical practitioner, who is providing the long-term care for these conditions should be sought. In many circumstances, the mere review of long-term medications and replacement with non ED promoting alternatives, often lead to improvement in ED. Family history of diabetes, hypertension and/or cardiovascular disease should enforce the proactive exclusion of these conditions at the outset of treatment; and thereafter during the course of long-term care. Some of these conditions are first diagnosed during the initial assessment for ED.

The evaluation provides an opportunity of health promotion for smoking, alcohol intake, diabetes, metabolic syndrome and cardiovascular disease.

The Evaluation of Erectile Dysfunction

The ease with which oral therapy for the treatment of erection dysfunction is becoming available has challenged the clinical need for invasive investigations. The investigations will continue to have a place in the subjective assessment of clinical trials and therapeutic studies. There continues to be a place for selective investigations when there is clinical evidence or suspicions of underlying organic aetiology for erectile dysfunction; and/or when there is a prospect of treating this cause. The indications for specific invasive diagnostic tests are declining. Specific investigations are indicated in non-psychogenic, non-organic primary ED, pelvic/ perineal vascular trauma, congenital penile curvature and Peyronies' disease, complex endocrine, psychiatric or psycho-sexual conditions, consideration of penile prosthesis and medico-legal investigations for sexual abuse.

1. Questionnaires

Questionnaires can provide an objective assessment for ED. They are indispensible in clinical trials; to objectively measure the effect of therapy. They provide a better objective assessment of ED before and after therapy. They are time demanding in a busy clinical setting. The clinician may overcome the time constraints during the consultation by providing the questionnaire to the patient to fill in, prior to the clinical visit. Investigations and treatment of ED in young man is better supported with questionnaires to objectively confirm the indication of therapy and assess the response, on follow-up.

The ability of the couple to discuss the findings of the questionnaire together first, and with the support of the clinician later can enhance the therapeutic effects. Most couples come with a defined problem of their won, which may fit into one of the stages of the sexual response cycle. Most patients give precise description of the problem, as they see it. The ability to obtain and maintain erection seems to be the most common complaint. Some patients complain of difficulty in ejaculation and others consider sexual desire as the main problem. Further question establish the patient's ability to achieve penetration, which is not usually volunteered prior to direct questions.

The International Index of Erectile Function (IIEF) is an elaborate questionnaire most suited to research situations and therapeutic trials. IIEF will provide objective assessment of the response to the therapy that is under investigation.

Androgen Deficiency in Aging Men (ADAM) questionnaire, lists 10 questions on the following areas: libido, lack of energy, decrease in strength and/or endurance, loss of weight, decline in life enjoyment, sadness or grumpiness, decline in rigidity and/or duration of erection, ability to play sport, falling asleep after dinner and work performance. It provide a generalised and overall performance assessment

2. Basic Haematological, Hormonal and Microbiological Investigations

The clinical examination should aim to exclude co-morbidities (e.g. blood pressure, athero- sclerosis, diabetes......). Primary care might have identified some of these conditions already; the treatment of which may have also contributed to the development of ED. A general cardiovascular, neurological and genital examination is an essential minimum; at least for the purpose of prescribing a systemic medication that may continue for the foreseeable future. The peripheral pulse (e.g. the first dorsal metatarsal arterial pulse), should give a fair indication about the integrity of peripheral small arteries, penile arteries included. The assessment of patients requires attention to the secondary sexual characteristics to exclude hypogonadism and to direct the relevant investigations.

The clinician need basic investigations first, including urinalysis, blood sugar and fasting lipid profiles; to exclude diabetes mellitus and/or dyslipidaemia, if not assessed in the previous 12 months.

Hormone profile, for testosterone, prolactin, de-hydro-epi-androsterone sulphate (DHEAS) should be considered. Bio-available or calculated free testosterone, from a morning blood sample is a better indication of hypogonadism; and should be repeated in another occasion.

Additional hormonal tests are considered in cases with proved low testosterone (e.g. prolactin, follicle stimulating hormone (FSH), luteinizing hormone (LH) and sex hormone binding globulin (SHBG)). These will help to differentiate between primary and secondary testosterone deficiency. Thyroid function tests, and free thyroxin, are required in selective cases.

Investigations to exclude sexually transmitted infections have a place in some cases. The clinician should discuss these tests with the patient; especially the one who is exploring sexual relationships with multiple changes of sexual partners.

3. Penile Angiography

Penile angiography continues to have a place in the diagnosis of isolated vascular occlusion in a young man. It is an essential test and a precursor for penile revascularisation procedure. It could also be used in selective cases of "Arterial Embolisation" in the treatment of high flow Priapism.

4. Nocturnal Penile Tumescence and Rigidity (NPTR) Measurement

Nocturnal erections, each lasting some 20-50 minutes, take place 4-6 times during the normal sleep cycle. The computerised measurement and recording of penile tumescence and rigidity during the sleep cycle provides a good measure on nocturnal erection status.

NPTR testing is a recognised method to differentiate between psychogenic and organic ED. NPTR test with a recorded 60% penile tip rigidity that lasts for 10 minutes or more, for at least 2 nights, indicates a functional erectile mechanism.

5. Cavernosometry and Cavernosography

Cavernosometry and Cavernosography have a narrow indication in identifying cases of arterial, cavernous tissue and/or veno-occlusive impairments. The principles involve the injection of the penile shaft with varying amounts of PGE_1, possibly with 1% local Lidocaine containing anaesthetic, then infusing a warm saline; to promote erection. The test requires recording the rate at which there is a decline in cavernous pressure from 150 mm Hg, within the following 30-60 seconds. It records the saline pressure at which erection could be re-achieved and the flow required to maintain erection.

Cavernosography involves the injection of a radio-active contrast agent and multiple penile x-ray pictures; in antero-posterior, lateral and oblique x-ray projections. Phenylephrine intra-cavernous injection achieves detumescence.

6. Intra-Cavernous Injection Test

The intra-cavernous-injection (ICI) test indicates a functional but not necessarily a normal erection; and therefore the information regarding the vascular status is rather limited. There had been claims that the ICI has a value in medico-legal investigations of cases of alleged sexual assault and rape; but erection may take place during the ICI test when it fails in normal circumstances. The main value of the test is to provide information regarding the potential success of self-administered intra-cavernous injection (ICI). Patients with arterial insufficiency or veno-occlusive dysfunction would respond positively to intra-cavernous injection.

7. Doppler Ultrasonography with Intra-Cavernous Injection Test

Doppler Ultrasonography is a reliable diagnostic test for penile arterial blood flow and cavernous function. Doppler ultrasonography of penile arteries with normal values obviates the need for extensive vascular investigations.

Management Strategy

The management of ED, in most cases, is symptomatic; to achieve erection and penile rigidity that is sustainable for satisfactory intercourse, for both patient and partner. In most cases, ED is treatable, but not curable. Curable cases include: psychogenic ED, primary testicular failure, hyper-prolactinaemia and/or pelvic trauma requiring penile revascularisation.

The majority of ED patients who require pharmacotherapy have no underlying direct cause for ED. Many ED patients have associated lifestyle and/or drug related factors that are amenable to modification and/or reversal. The patient needs to undertake a strategy for lifestyle and risk factor modification. Sedentary life, excessive alcohol drinking and lipid imbalance perpetuates the existing ED and promotes future worsening. The Lipidaemia modifying therapy may unfortunately contribute to sexual dysfunction.

The main factors affecting the choice of ED treatment modality are acceptability, side-effects, efficacy, safety, invasiveness and/or cost. The clinician has a role and responsibility for health education and prevention; not only the therapeutic management of ED. S/HE should also carefully review the side-effects and possible alternatives for prescription drugs that may precipitate and/or promote ED. Patient's indulgence of non-prescription and recreational drugs that promote ED is more challenging; especially when the patient decides to continue with these drugs. The benefit of lifestyle changes reflect on co-morbid metabolic diseases (e.g. diabetes, hyper-lipidaemia...) and/or cardiovascular diseases (e.g. hypertension). There is therefore an overall dual benefit both ED and general health.

ED initiates a cycle of loss of confidence and anxiety, which perpetuates the impotence in a vicious circle. An important part of the clinician's role is to break this cycle. It is important that the clinician assures the patient on normal examination and test results; and provide explanation and advice on the role of incidental observations.

Psychogenic ED requires psychosexual therapy, in association with oral treatment, vacuum devices or ICI to rebuild confidence. The clinician should agree a weaning off programme with the young patients who undertakes oral ED pharmacotherapy, as a supportive treatment for psychogenic ED. This early agreement will help to promote the patient's confidence and avoid unnecessary long term drug usage. The patient could be advised to attempt sexual intercourse, on occasions, without the prior use of the drugs. Hopefully this will gradually rebuild his confidence and reduce dependence on the drug therapy. The clinician needs the support of psychosexual counselling team to manage the conditions of patients with significant psychological problems.

The Treatment Options for Erectile Dysfunction

A practical measure of the efficacy ED therapy is its ability to produce and maintain erection; that is rigid, persistent and satisfactory for sexual intercourse. Different patient oriented questionnaires are available to measure these points objectively and in a numerical manner. *The international index of erectile dysfunction (IIEF),* questions the domains of erection, orgasm, sexual desire, sexual satisfaction and overall satisfaction. It provides fifteen questions on the five point scale. It provides a cut point to identify ED. The *sexual encounter profile (SEP)* refers to five questions on: erection, penile-vaginal insertion, time span of erection, satisfaction with erection and satisfaction with the sexual experience. The general SEP questions regarding "satisfactory erection" are non-specific and do not provide objective assessment of therapeutic efficacy. Studies estimate that one in five ED patients request medical assistance. The reasons may be embarrassment, lack of interest, personal distractions and/or therapy cost.

1. Oral Therapy

Oral pharmacotherapy is becoming the first line of treatment for ED. The clinician needs to assess the therapeutic outcome; namely penile rigidity and time span of erection, drug side effects and the partner's satisfaction with therapy. Patient reports of oral therapy success are usually high. Combination therapy could be considered when a sole drug treatment proves unsuccessful; following 3-4 attempts of adequate intake.

Patients seeking sexual activity should have the benefit of frank, calculated and objective discussion regarding cardiovascular disease and risk category. The high risk cardiovascular system conditions include: uncontrolled hypertension, moderate to severe valve disease, high risk arrhythmia, unstable angina, refractory angina, recent myocardial infarction, congestive heart failure and/or left ventricular dysfunction. The low risk category include patients with uncomplicated past myocardial infarction, mild or stable angina, asymptomatic coronary artery disease, controlled hypertension and/or mild valve diseases. The low risk category patient should be able to perform moderate intensity exercise without cardiac symptoms. There is no indication for cardiac stress tests prior to resumption of sexual activity in a patient within this group of low risk category.

A) Phosphodiesterase-5 (PDE-5) Inhibitors

The cavernous smooth muscle Cyclic Guanosine Monophosphate (cGMP) is a second messenger and plays a key factor in erection. There are several PDEs, of which PDE-5 is the most abundant in the corpus cavernosum. It is converted into a biologically inactive mono-phosphate by the hydrolysis of its phospho-diesterase bond, rendering it physiologically inactive. PDE-5 inhibitors extend the physiological action of cGMP, as a secondary messenger and intermediary in erection.

PDE-5 inhibitors have a good track record for efficacy in ED whether psychogenic, neuro-genic (e.g. diabetes, neurological disorders and spinal cord injuries and multiple sclerosis) or vasculo-genic (e.g. radical pelvic surgery with nerve sparing procedures) or patients with renal insufficiency. The most commonly encountered side-effects are: headache, rhinitis and/or dyspepsia. Rarely, patients complain of visual disturbances, with Sildenafil. The same side-effects take place with overdosing.

PDE-5 inhibitors are contraindicated in patients who are undertaking nitrate-containing drugs, whether short or long acting, including recreational drugs and nitrous oxide (NO) donors. PDE-5 inhibitors have no clinically relevant drug interactions with all classes of anti-hypertensives. Their use with alcohol intake does not lead to significant hypotension; despite their concurrent peripheral vasodilatation. The practical difficulty comes with the use of emergency nitrate medications in a patient who has already undertaken PDE-5 inhibitor. If the interval is more than 24 hours for Sildenafil and Vardenafil, and more than 48 hours for Tadalafil, the use of nitrate medication is likely to be safe. If there is a necessity of nitrate medication within this timeframe, then medical supervision should be at hand.

The clinician needs to exercise caution in using the drugs in patients with hepatic and/or renal failure and to those with known risks of Priapism (e.g. leukaemia, sickle cell disease and multiple myeloma). The drugs are better avoided in patients who have had recent myocardial infarction, arrhythmia, stroke or left ventricular outflow obstruction. Patients undertaking α blockers (e.g. for benign prostatic hyperplasia), could be at risk of postural hypotension. The clinician should consult the interaction tables for the drugs under question.

There is no clinically significant compromise of the bleeding time, in patients taking aspirin, warfarin or heparin.

Cytochrome P_{450} 3A4 (CYP 3A4) inhibitors like Erythromycin, Ketoconazole, Itraconazole and Protease inhibitors (e.g. Saquinavior, Indinavir and Ritonavir) compete with PDE-5 inhibitors for metabolism and consequently increase the plasma levels; which may reach a tenfold increase.

Sildenafil (25, 50 and 100mg) tablets, Tadalafil (10 and 20mg) tablets and Vardenafil (5, 10 and 20mg) tablets are licensed for use "on demand" basis. Tadalafil 2.5 and 5mg tablets are licensed for daily usage. The longer half life of Tadalafil (i.e. the time interval from maximal to half plasma concentration) indicates that it would still be available for the patient's sexual activity for some day and a half after intake.

Clinical significance

The clinician should differentiate between actual therapeutic failures and delayed drug absorption. The intake of a high fat content meal delays gastric emptying; and consequently the drug action. This proves to be a common cause for perceived "drug failure".

The clinician should review any concurrent anti-hypertensive therapy and avoid drugs notorious of inducing ED. The concomitant treatment of hypercholesterolemia and subsequent reduction in low density lipoproteins (LDL) may improve the therapeutic efficacy of PDE5-inhibitors; due to the reduction in the LDL negative effects on endothelial function.

Daily dosing or doubling the maximum dosage proves successful in a considerable number of cases that failed to respond on routine dosages. Daily dosing is clinically indicated for "sexual rehabilitation"; following nerve sparing procedures for radical prostatectomy. Tadalafil (2.5mg and 5mg tablets) are available for daily dosing.

Nitrates are contraindicated with PDE5 inhibitors. Combined together, PDE5 inhibitor and nitrates can cause unpredictable fall in blood pressure. This should be amply clarified to patients who may obtain the ED drugs from internet suppliers; without the knowledge or recourse of their own family doctor. The clinician should explicitly advise the patient against recreational nitrate-containing drugs (e.g. poppers). A practical difficulty arises in encountering a patient suffering an anginal attack; whilst taking PDE 5 inhibitor. Nitro-glycerine is better avoided for twenty-four hours after Sildenafil and Vardenafil, or forty-eight hours following Tadalafil intake. There appears to be no evidence that PDE5 inhibitors increase the risk of myocardial infarction rates in patients who received these drugs. A small additional drop in blood pressure may take place on using PDE5 inhibitors with other antihypertensive agents (e.g. calcium blockers, angiotensin converting enzyme inhibitors, angiotensin receptor blockers, beta blockers and/or diuretics). The patient should declare PDE 5 inhibitor, as a drug, during any medical history and enquiry about "medications".

PDE5 inhibitors may interact with alpha blockers (e.g. during the treatment of benign prostatic hyperplasia). The local pharmacopeia's advice should guide the management. Some combinations are absolutely contraindicated and others require a clearance period of more than four hours. Consideration for testosterone replacement therapy is helpful to patients with evident hypogonadism.

Therapeutic Failures

- Patients with cavernous insufficiency, known also as veno-occlusive dysfunction, represent a challenge due to failure of response to PDE-5 inhibitors or ICI.
- Autonomic penile nerve supply damage, due to pelvic surgery or trauma, lead to lack of responsiveness to PDE-5 inhibitors. The patient requires an alternative (e.g. Trans-urethral Alprostadil or ICI).

B) Korean Red Ginseng

Korean red ginseng has proven erection promoting effect; but its mechanism of action is not clear.

C) Trazodone

Psychiatrists managing patients with depressive illness and ED may consider Trazodone. Its erection inducing properties are due to, which has α Adrenoceptor blockage and cavernous smooth muscle relaxation. It also acts centrally, as serotonin re-uptake inhibitor. The severity of its side-effects can lead to discontinuation of therapy. The patient may experience a sense of fatigue, dizziness, sleepiness, headache and/or nausea.

D) Yohimbine

Yohimbine is an alkaloid extract from the Yohimbehe tree park. It has a central and peripheral α_2 adrenergic antagonistic activity; and peripheral sympathetic and penile arterial activity. Centrally, it blocks the erection inhibiting impulses. Peripherally, it counteracts epinephrine and nor-epinephrine vaso-constriction and reduction in penile arterial blood flow. A dosage of 5 – 15 mg, three times daily, for six to eight weeks is required to improve erection in non organic ED. On need use, of 15 mg, some 2 to 3 hours prior to the intended sexual activity, may have a place in cases; where there had been no response or distressing side effects to other oral therapies. The side effects are mostly sympatho-mimetic (e.g. anxiety, tachycardia, palpitation, diarrhoea, sleeplessness, restlessness, agitation and, more seriously, manic symptoms). It is contraindicated in patients with uncontrolled hypertension, angina pectoris, myocardial infarction, psychiatric disorders and/or undertaking Tricyclic antidepressants. It is better avoided in hypertensive patients, as it may lead to additional increase in blood pressure.

E) Apomorphine

Apomorphine is a dopamine agonist that acts centrally to enhance the sexual stimulation cascade. It has a licence, for the treatment of ED, in some countries,. The patient undertakes 2 or 3 mg, sublingual tablets, on demand, some 20-30 minutes before attempting sexual intercourse. The patient may experience nausea, headache and/or dizziness. They are usually self-limiting; but occasionally severe enough to require cessation of treatment. There has been rare reporting of syncope. If tolerable, the drug is usually safe to use in parallel with antihypertensive drugs and/or nitrates; which provide a practical advantage over PDE5 inhibitors in patients taking nitrates.

2. Intra-Cavernous Injection (ICI)

The injections of vasoactive drugs, into penile cavernous tissue, to induce erection represented a milestone in the management of erectile dysfunction; whether psychogenic, vasculo-genic or neuro-genic. ICI drug leads to relaxation of the smooth muscles of the cavernous tissue and penile arteries, leading to sinusoidal engorgement, to the point of compression of subtunical veins and veno-occlusion.

The Clinician needs to discuss the technique of ICI with the patient first to overcome any mental barrier against its use. S/he should provide a training session, to explain the principle and technique of introducing the drug. S/he may use a complimentary diagram or model, showing a longitudinal and cross section of the penile shaft, site and depth of injection. The patient needs to avoid too superficial or too deep injections. Two to three site injections, on each side, followed by self penile massage, would help disseminating the drug into the cavernous tissue. The atmosphere of the surrounding clinical room should be private and relaxed, but with some degree of clinical supervision at hand. The patient should avoid anxiety and sympathetic autonomic overstimulation. The most common complication is penile haematoma.

A) Papaverine

Papaverine is a smooth muscle relaxant of the cavernous sinusoids, penile arteries in direct effect. It reduces the adrenergic nerves induced smooth muscle stimulation. It acts via phospho-diesterase inhibitor, increasing the intracellular cAMP cGMP. It suppresses the angiotensin II secretion. It causes inhibition of L-type Ca^{2+} channels, leading to cavernosal engorgement and penile erection. There is a risk of penile fibrosis in one of ten users, due to a cytotoxic effect on cavernosal endothelial cells. The drug is still available in cost conscious settings, and used in dosages ranging from 10 to 100 mg (most commonly 30 – 60 mg).

B) Alpha-Adrenoceptor Blocking Agents

1) Prostaglandin E1 (PGE1)/ Alprostadil

Alprostadil is a smooth muscle relaxant. It acts by attachment to a cell membrane receptor and leading to intracellular increase in cAMP and inhibition of nor-adrenalin release. Clinical use indicates less complications with cavernosal fibrosis or Priapism, than Papaverine and/or Phentolamine. Some patients complain of a feeling of intra-penile tension, which is likely to be due excessive engorgement. The availability of dual chamber syringes, in concentrations ranging from 10, 20 and 40 μg, has improved the ease and technique of self injections.

2) Phentolamine

Phentolamine is competitive non-selective A_1 and A_2 adreneoceptor blocker that acts on both pre-synaptic and post-synaptic sites. Its use in conjunction with Papaverine has an additive effect with better efficiency, more penile rigidity and longer standing erections, than if either drug is used alone.

C) Combination of Papaverine and Phentolamine

Combination of Papaverine and Phentolamine proved effective in inducing and maintaining erections sufficient for intercourse. Its availability was advantageous in the era before Alprostadil ICI. It carries more risk of

Priapism and cavernous fibrosis. It may still have a place, in patients when PGE_1 proves ineffective; or those who suffer penile tension with PGE_1.

3. Intra-urethral Prostaglandin E1/ Alprostadil

Transurethral Alprostadil (PGE_1) provides an alternative to ICI. Autonomic penile nerve supply damage, due to pelvic surgery or trauma, leading to lack of responsiveness to PDE-5 inhibitors, is the main indication of transurethral Alprostadil. Urethral pain is the most common complaint and affects of one in four patients. Feeling of dizziness and syncope is rare; but could be a cause of concern for both the patient and clinician.

4. Vacuum Erection Devices (VED)

Vacuum Erection Devices (VED) promotes passive engorgement of the corporae cavernousae; followed by the application of a constriction ring, to retain blood within the corporae. They are efficient, easy to use, have limited side-effects and long safety history. They require cooperation, understanding, support and motivation, of both partners. Men, in stable partnerships, are more likely to accept the device, than those who are courting and in new relationships. Patients report high efficiency but variable degrees of satisfaction, regardless of the ED cause. Reports of dissatisfactions appear usually within the first three months. Their popularity had declined due to competition with oral therapy for ED. VED is contraindicated in patients at risk of Priapism or Peyronie's disease, whether congenital or acquired.

The success of VED depends on the extent and clarity of instructions, on how to use it, rather than the aetiology of ED. There is better outcome when the Clinician instructs the patient on VED use and allows him to practice, under supervision. VED could be used for ED of any underlying aetiology; or when there is apprehension in using other methods of ED treatment. Their immediate effect provides a practical value for patients wanting timely erection. It is suitable for those conscious of the expense of oral therapy. Oral therapy, in conjunction with VED, for the treatment of ED could prove successful; when either method was successful previously but declined later. VED could be used with ICI, to improve its efficacy. VED has a place as an alternative to oral therapy or when ICI is contraindicated.

The VED device is made of a plastic cylinder attached to vacuum producing pump. The pump is either connected to the cylinder via a tube or integrated in the end and battery operated. The patient applies a lubricant gel to the lower end of the cylinder and holds it firmly pressed against his body, to make it airtight. The vacuum pressure draws blood into the cavernous bodies of the penis. The patient then rolls off the rubber constriction ring, from the cylinder on to the base of the penis, to prevent blood leakage. The patient will find it easier to achieve better erection if he applies the process while he is standing.

The suction process creates negative pressure, leading to gradual engorgement of the penis. The application of the elastic ring around the penile base obstructs the release of blood and leads to penile rigidity. The apparatus must contain a pressure regulator; as excessive negative pressure can lead to bruises and haematoma. The clinician should ensure that a prescribed VED should have a valid Medical devices licence. A prolonged constriction, by the rubber band, can lead to ischemia. The clinician should warn the patient not to fall asleep, following sexual intercourse, and overlooking the timely removal of the constriction band. The device independence on intact arterial inflow is an advantage; which extends its use to patients with peripheral vascular disease.

The penile crurae are not engorged and will not support penile- vaginal intromission. The patient will need manual assistance to achieve penile-vaginal insertion. A third of patients using VED report ejaculatory difficulty. Many complain of painful ejaculation, as a result of the urethral blockage, caused by the constriction ring. Penile numbness, bruises and/or petechiae are occasional problems. Skin petechiae may lead to skin hyper-pigmentation. Patients who become dissatisfied with the device report unnatural, cyanotic and cooler penile erection and increase in glans volume.

5. Surgical Treatment of Erectile Dysfunction

A) Penile Vascular Surgery

The improvement in vascular micro surgical techniques have progressed penile revascularization procedures. The procedures involve the anastomosis of the inferior epigastric artery into the dorsal penile arteries, to improve revascularisation. The procedure is suitable for the young healthy patient, who has had compromised penile arterial supply, due to pelvic or straddle trauma.

The procedures are not suitable for patients who have generalised vascular disease (e.g. systemic atherosclerosis).

The procedures follow three principle surgical techniques: anastomosis of the inferior epigastric artery with the dorsal penile arteries, with the deep dorsal vein of penis or with both deep dorsal vein and deep dorsal artery. The measure of success is the patient's ability to obtain and maintain satisfactory erection; following sexual stimulation.

Surgical procedures for the management of dysfunctional penile veno-occlusive conditions are a source of conflicting reports. There is no agreement on their indications, the best surgical techniques and/or outcome results. Venus ligation, resection and Embolisation techniques have their proponents and opponents. Some surgeons have tried more extensive procedures like extensive exposure and excision of the deep dorsal vein of the penis, posterior ligation or crural plication.

B) Penile Prosthetic Surgery

Penile prosthetic surgery aims to implant either a semi-rigid or inflatable device into the corporae cavernosae; to emulate erection and rigidity and to enable the patient to engage in coital activity.

The semi-rigid, or malleable, penile prosthesis gives the patient the ability to position it manually in a straight direction, to engage in sexual intercourse, or downward direction, for micturition and dressing. The malleable prosthesis is not suitable for patients who are potential candidates for future glans and/or urethral surgery. They are not suitable for transurethral surgery or those who have future indications for repeated Cysto-urethro-scopy (e.g. follow-up for bladder tumours). Those who have no penile sensation (e.g. patients with spinal chord injuries) are at risk of pressure necrosis. Some patients find them difficult to conceal.

The inflatable penile prostheses consist of a pair of intra-corporal devices and a scrotal pump/ reservoir, connected by tubing. By squeezing the pump, the intra-penile cylinders are inflated to achieve an erect position. For deflation, the patient squeezes a release cap to deflate the two cylinders.

A three piece inflatable prosthesis has a separate reservoir that is implanted in the retro-pubic space. The patient squeezes the scrotal pump to cause inflation of the intra-penile cylinders and achieve erection. To deflate the implant, he activates the release bar, which is part of the scrotal pump. It has the additional advantage of increase in penile size when the prosthesis is inflated. The flaccid state of inflatable prosthesis allows good concealment which is not possible with the semi-rigid types. They require some degree of dexterity and therefore may not be suitable for every patient (e.g. Parkinson 's disease or severe rheumatoid deformity).

Patient selection and matching with the prosthesis type requires a careful consideration of the patient's existing disease conditions, clinical status and future progress. It provides an alternative choice to couples; especially those who did not benefit from alternative treatment methods. The surgeon's experience and meticulous techniques determine the outcome, functionality, patient satisfaction and future need for revision surgery. Like most devices, mechanical failures may take place, which would require revised surgery. In line with other prostheses, infection is a possibility; which may require removal. Reinsertion of replacement prosthesis, following an interim period, is fraught with technical difficulties; which is aggravated by fibrosis following the first operation. A salvage procedures, which involves removal of the first prosthesis and reinsertion of another one is preferable.

Lack of penile shaft and glans engorgement is a source of dissatisfaction to some couples undertaking penile prosthesis surgery only. Combination of prosthesis with PDE5 inhibitors, improves the penile shaft and glans engorgement and brings it close to natural erection.

Chapter VII

Ejaculatory Dysfunctions

Ejaculatory disorders include premature ejaculation, inhibited ejaculation, an-ejaculation, anorgasmia, retrograde ejaculation and painful ejaculation. The ejaculatory function involves a process of emission, ejection and orgasm. Emission is initiated by genital and/or cerebral erotic stimuli leading to a sympathetic spinal cord reflex and contraction of accessory sexual organs. There is a degree of voluntary control on emission, which is considerable at the beginning of the process; but declines gradually, to a point when ejaculation is inevitable. Ejection involves bladder neck closure, in association with rhythmic contractions of pelvic floor muscles and relaxation of the external urinary sphincter. It is mainly a sympathetic spinal reflex; with no voluntary controls. Orgasm is the cerebral appreciation of the sensory stimuli arising from the posterior urethra, vera montanum and accessory sexual organs. Serotenergic and dopaminergic neurones dominate the control of the ejaculatory reflex; with secondary involvement of other neurones. Animal, human, sexual, psychological and pharmacological studies suggest that Serotenergic neurones have a role in premature ejaculation.

Premature Ejaculation (PE)

Premature ejaculation is identified on the patient's complaint and/or the partner's history of "recurrent ejaculation on or shortly after attempted penetration, over which the man has little or no voluntary control and leading to distress to one or both partners, or lack of enjoyment in lovemaking". The study of time interval between attempted intromission and ejaculation, otherwise known as *Inter-vaginal Ejaculatory Latency Time (IELT),* provides objective measure and best suited to therapeutic drug trials. There are parameters, to define PE, in terms of a prescribed time spans (e.g. ejaculation within 2 minutes of penetration). According to the time sensitive definition ejaculation within 1 min is regarded as severe PE. Masters and Johnson initially defined PE as "the man's inability to control and defer ejaculation, until the female partner was sexually satisfied; on at least 50% of intercourse attempts". Understandably, the condition will come to medical attention, when both or either partners, is suffering distress. The couple's complaint should be the physician's primary interest, rather than the prescribed time scale. In *primary PE,* the patient complains of PE since coitarche; as compared to *secondary or acquired PE,* which occurs at a later stage of sex life, following a problem free interval. *Global PE* involves all sex partners, whilst *Situational PE* relates to an individual partner, but not another.

Studies suggest a higher incidence of PE in men of Middle Eastern and Asian origin than Caucasian; and in Caucasians than Afro-Caribbean's. The PE patients don't usually report reduced sexual desire or reduced arousability. The extent of sexual dis-satisfaction impinges on the coupes presentation for medical help. Distress plays an important role in couples seeking assistance. The female partner is usually more distressed and complainant. Tables to measures of IELT, sexual satisfaction, voluntary control and/or distress are objective parameters for the diagnosis and assessment of response to treatment, in therapeutic clinical trials. In clinical practice, the assessment is subjective. Couples who seek help for PE deserve medical attention.

The diagnosis is based on the patient's clinical and sexual history; which directs the examination and investigations to exclude concurrent conditions (e.g. prostatitis, hypo and hyper thyroidism and cerebro-vascular accident). PE may accompany other erectile dysfunctions or interpersonal conflicts between the partners.

The Management of Couple Presenting with PE

A) Stop-Start Programme

- *Stage I:* The patient stimulates his penis, manually, up to the point of high arousal and short of ejaculation; then he stops stimulation until arousal subsides. He resumes stimulation again to the point of arousal;

then he stops stimulation. The sequence of stimulation and stopping continues for several times; before it ends in ejaculation. The patient repeats the exercise several times during the week; with the aim of gradually increasing the duration of stimulation he can achieve before the need to stop.

- *Stage II:* The partner applies identical steps of the stimulation exercise, to be guided by the patient on when to stop and when to start.
- *Stage III:* The couple practice penile-vaginal intromission, without thrusting, aiming for the man to learn about enjoying copulation.
- *Stage IV:* The couple practice penile-vaginal intromission, with thrusting, up to the point of imminent ejaculation, then stopping before ejaculation.
- *Stage V:* The exercise is repeated up to the point of ejaculation.

The couple should repeat each stage several times, before moving to the next. The programme requires cooperation between the couple; who have good interaction with the therapist.

B) Sensate Focus Programme

The sensate focus programme, running in parallel with the stop-start programme, carries the advantage of satisfying the partner's sexual needs. It also helps to direct the man's focus away from his genitalia, in the ejaculatory process.

C) Penile Glans Squeeze Technique

The couple apply the same stages of the stop-start programme, with squeezing the glans penis, between two fingers and thumb, at the highest point of arousal, until it subsides. The man applies the penile glans squeeze in the first stage; then the woman, in stage 2, 3, 4 and 5.

D) Topical Anaesthetic

Topical anaesthetics (e.g. Prilocaine or Lidocaine), in the form of spray, gel or cream are becoming widely available as non-prescription treatment. The clinician should advise the couple on using condoms to avoid the partner's exposure to the drugs.

E) Psychotherapy

Psychotherapy is required for cases when PE is precipitated by interpersonal difficulties. The clinician should be alert to this need and direct the referral.

F) Pharmaco-Therapy

Selective Serotonin Reuptake Inhibitors (SSRIs) are advantageous in the treatment of PE. The clinician should be well acquainted with their use and side effects and avoid using the drugs for PE in patients with bipolar depression. She/he should warn the patient that the drug is not prescribed for depression; as some patients get alarmed on reading the "patient information sheet". The clinician should consider "on demand" treatment initially. Paroxetine seems to cause acceptable delay in ejaculation. Alternatively, Clomipramine, or Sertraline is efficacious in delaying ejaculation, with no or minimal side effects. Daily treatment should be considered if the "on demand" therapy is not satisfactory.

G) Phospho-diesterase Type 5 Inhibitors

PDE-5 inhibitors may be advantageous in patients with associated erectile dysfunction who have secondary PE.

Delayed Ejaculation (DE)

Secondary DE may be part of an ageing process, prostate or bladder neck surgery, abuse of alcohol, thiazide diuretics, hypogonadism and/or anti-depressants . They may act as single or cumulative aetiological factors in precipitating and aggravating DE. Primary DE is rare, but would suggest either a congenital bladder neck or pelvic floor problem. Rarely, there is a deep rooted psychogenic factor. DE assessment should include the patient's detailed history about masturbation. Auto-sexual orientation, frequent and aggressive masturbation would influence the man's desire, fantasies and erection. It can create disparity between his experience with masturbation and partner-related sexual intercourse. The underlying problem may be a difficulty, in psychosexual arousal, during partner-related versus fantasy situations. Self realisation of this situation may lead to anxiety, autonomic sympathetic overstimulation, inhibited ejaculation and lack of orgasm. The management should be tailored to the underlying aetiology.

A) Sex Education

Sex education aims to target auto-sexual activity and masturbation. The aim is to reduce the patient's anxiety that is resulting from the disparity between achievement during masturbation and partner related sexual activity. The sensate focus programme should improve the partner related sexual activity; whilst the patient is aiming to reduce performance related anxiety.

B) Desensitisation Programme

The programme is best suited to patients who have partner-related and situational DE.

- *Stage I:* The man masturbates in the absence of his partner first; whilst imagining her presence or involvement; to achieve and enjoy arousal; without the focus and need to ejaculate. The goal is to promote the psychogenic element of arousal and to fantasise about his partner, in her absence. .
- *Stage II:* The patient continues with self stimulation in the proximity of his partner, but without her direct involvement. The aim is promote his fantasy about her and her involvement, in her presence. The exercise is repeated, for the patient to reach arousal, in the presence of his partner; to the point when ejaculation becomes inevitable.
- *Stage III:* The same steps are followed whilst the partner is in close proximity to the patient, but not involved in the initial stimulation stage. At the point of arousal, the partner takes over the stimulation, till ejaculation; without intromission.
- *Stage IV:* The patient starts stimulation whilst the partner is sitting astride him. She takes stimulation and intromission; just before ejaculation, for ejaculation to take place between the vulval labiae. The exercise is repeated several times, on different occasions and different situations.
- *Stage V:* The partners follow the same procedures and ending with vaginal intromission and ejaculation in the vagina.

C) Pharmacotherapy

Pharmacotherapy in the management of DE, is disadvantaged by the lack of double blind placebo controlled investigations. *5-Hydroxy Tryptamine (5-HT) receptor antagonists* (e.g. Cyproheptadine) may be effective. *Central and peripheral dopaminergic drugs* (e.g. Amantadine and Apomorphine) increase the dopamine activity, sexual behaviour and ejaculation. *Yohimbine* (α-1 dopamine agonist and α-2 antagonist) reverses the anorgasmia that is drug induced. *Dopamine reuptake inhibitors* (e.g. Bupropion) reverses the SSRI induced anorgasmia. Buspirone (5-HT$_{1A}$ receptor agonist) may resolve anxiety related sexual dysfunction. The dosages require tailoring, in balance with the patient's drug induced negative side-effects.

Retarded Ejaculation (RE) and An-Ejaculation

Ejaculation requires the functional closure of the bladder neck and proximal urethra, to propel semen in a forward direction. The most common causes for RE encountered in clinical practice are diabetic autonomic neuropathy, transurethral and open prostatectomy. Congenital bladder neck dysfunction is rare cause; but should be excluded in patients with primary RE. Other surgical procedures that may cause disruption of the autonomic sympathetic neural supply to the bladder neck (e.g. Retro-peritoneal lymphadenectomy and colorectal surgery), and spinal cord injury also lead to RE. Drugs causing paralysis of the bladder neck will lead to RE; namely: *al-blocking agents* (e.g. Tamsulosin, Terazosin, Prazosin and Alfuzosin), *Anti hypertensives* (e.g. Clonidine, Phenoxypenzamine and thiazide diuretics), *Anti-depressants and some anti-psychotics* (e.g. Chlorpromazine, Levo-mepromazine). The patient may be using more than one of these drugs at the same time.

A history of past surgical procedure may lead the diagnosis to the underlying cause. Post ejaculatory urine analysis and microscopy tests will demonstrate sperms in urine and confirms the clinical suspicion. The finding of some 5 to 10 sperms/ high power field is diagnostic.

Pharmacotherapy is beneficial when there is a need for a functional achievement (e.g. desire to father children). Otherwise, clinical experience suggests that it is unlikely for the patient to continue on long term drug treatment. If therapy is required, the options are ephedrine, pseudo-ephedrine, and Tricyclic anti-depressant with anti-cholinergic effects (e.g. Desipramine or Imipramine). The treatment should be used 2 or 3 hours before ejaculation.

Painful Ejaculation (Odyn-orgasmia)

Painful ejaculation is a distressing complaint and may affect patients suffering from acute or chronic prostatitis, seminal vesiculitis or benign prosthetic hypertrophy (BPH). Calculi in the seminal vesicle or obstruction of the ejaculatory duct are rare but treatable causes. It is rarely encountered in patients taking Tricyclic anti-depressants and SSRIs; due to the ensuing sympathetic block and bladder neck dysfunction; when dosage readjustment may resolve the problem.

Chapter VIII

Peyronie's Disease (PD) and Acquired Penile Curvature

Peyronie's disease (PD) is characterised by penile curvature, penile pain and erectile dysfunction. Louis XV's Royal Surgeon, Francoise de la Peyronie, described the condition as "rosary beads of scar tissue extending along the dorsum of the penis and upward penile curvature during erection." Earlier medical literature described similar conditions. PD is caused by fibrotic plaques that develop in the tunica albuginea of the penis. It is typically dorsal and uni-focal; but may be lateral or rarely ventral. The plaques cause shortening of the relevant strip of the tunica albuginea with consequent curvature during erection and penile shortening or deformity. In the early stage, there is inflammatory process associated with pain which may last for months with progressive deformity. Patients experience pain mostly during erection but some give history during flaccidity. Lack of pain suggests stable disease, plaque and deformity. Middle aged and elderly men present with PD as their main complaint. The level of anxiety seems to be higher with younger men, who are courting as compared to older men in a stable relationship. The partner's response can have impact on the patient's reaction and request for medical care. There are associated risk factors, namely hypertension, hyperuricaemia and hyper-cholesterolaemia. Its incidence in the population varies between 1-2% and there are claims of higher incidence. A third of PD patients have evidence of other connective disease disorders.

PD is a connective tissue disease leading to derangement of the tunica albuginea. It is currently considered as a wound healing disorder in response to penile trauma; with imbalance between pro and anti-fibrotic factors due to genetic predisposition. It is characterised by disorganised excessive collagen and extra-cellular matrix, loss and fragmentation of elastic fibres and fibrin deposits. There is increased ratio of Type-III to Type-I collagen and increased density of fibroblasts and inflammatory infiltrate of lymphocytes and plasma cells. The tunica albuginea loses flexibility due to the abnormal matrix and elasticity. Genetic predisposition, heightened response to traumatic inflammation, familial history, association with Dupuytren's contraction, HLA-B7 and HLA-B27 and auto-immune mechanism are postulated and continue to be explored. Trauma leading to extra-vasation of fibrin is thought to trigger the process. This theory was supported by the induction of similar changes by the injection of fibrin into the tunica albuginea of rodents.

Doppler ultrasonography studies suggest that arterial insufficiency plays a major role in patient's suffering ED; helped by the venous dysfunction resulting from a deformed tunica albuginea. The excessive curvature may add to a mechanical ED; aided by patient's own anxiety or partner's additional pressure.

The diagnosis is based on the patient's history, some of whom come with self-taken photographs, indicating the extent and direction of deformity during erection. The clinical history should aim to exclude associated conditions and proactively inquire about erectile dysfunction and/or dyspareunia experienced by the partners. The characteristics of ED, difficulty in intromission, generalised lack of tumescence and/or poor tumescence distal to the plaque should be identified. These parameters will direct the management. Colour Doppler ultrasonography, following induction of erection with the injection of intra-cavernosal vaso-active agent (e.g. Alprostadil), should precede surgical correction. Straightening procedures are indicated in a patient with preserved erectile function; penile prosthesis is likely to benefit those with ED.

Conservative treatment is indicated in the early, painful, progressive, unstable disease and/or mild curvatures. Most senior patients decline surgical intervention; if the degree of curvature is stable and does not interfere with sexual intercourse. *Oral Vitamin E* may act through its antioxidant properties. A high dosage of 800-1000 mg daily is associated with pain reduction. There is no evidence that it has an effect in reducing already existing deformity. *Oral Colchicine* induces collagenase activity and reduces collagen synthesis; but no evidence in reducing already existing deformity. *Intralesional Steroids* have anti-inflammatory, fibrin and collagen reduction properties. There is no evidence of objective change in plaque size. There is increased risk of tissue atrophy, loss of planes and compromise of surgical repair procedures.

Intralesional Verapamil injection (10mg/ 6cc of saline) is mediated by its effects on fibroblasts and cytokine inhibition. The regimen requires two weekly injections, for a total of 6 months. It makes scientific sense but there are no placebo controlled trials. *Intralesional Collagenase injection* had reports of improvement of curvature and patients satisfaction. *Penile traction devices and Vacuum therapy* have its proponents who report variable degrees of success. *Local Penile Lithotripsy* should be considered with caution, due to lack of long term outcome measures; especially its effects on cavernosal tissue. Younger patients usually request surgical reconstruction.

Reconstructive surgery should only be attempted after a year of stable disease; to allow for disease stability. It should be reserved for severe deformities which occur in 10% of patients with ED. Tonical shortening surgical procedures are acceptable for cases with mild curvature (i.e. less than 60 degrees). Plication of the contra-lateral point to that of the plaque is suitable for lateral curvatures but promotes penile shortening. In case with severe curvature (i.e. more than 60 degrees), tunical lengthening procedures are preferable to avoid additional penile shortening. High-grade curvature benefits most from plaque excision and grafting. Associated ED should be managed first with oral or injectable vaso-active agents. Penile prosthesis implantation is reserved for cases with unsuccessful response to ED therapy, severe deformity and/ or severe curvature. The success rate of oral or injectable vaso-active agents is variable; especially in patients suffering co-morbidities (e.g. Diabetes or hypertension).

Tunical lengthening procedures involves incision or partial excision and grafting; at the site of maximum curvature. Tunical shortening procedures include: excision and closure, plication alone or plaque incision and plication. The patient's condition and surgeon's preference direct the choice of surgical techniques. There is no evidence that one surgical procedure is more superior or successful than the other. Post surgical rehabilitation should start early postoperatively; with daily massage and manual stretch. It could be supported with intake of PDE-5 inhibitors, to encourage nocturnal erections.

Congenital Penile Curvature is the result of inborn abnormality of the penile ventral fascia, corpus spongiosum or both. It may be the result of arrest in normal development, testosterone deficiency or insensitivity. The correction is surgical; by lengthening the short side of the fascia or shortening the long side. The rate of success is high with rare ED complications in later life.

Chapter IX

Priapism

Priapism describes penile erection that is lasting for several hours, not related to continued sexual stimulation and does not subside following orgasm. The name originated from the myth of a Greek god Priapus, protector of male genitalia. The Greeks depicted Priapus on fresco paintings with a permanently erect penis.

Ischemic Low blood flow Priapism is associated with blockage of the deep penile veins. It presents with fully rigid corporae-cavernosae and penile pain. There may have been a recent history of intra-cavernosal injection (ICI), for the treatment of impotence. The patient may have had a history of recurrent episodes of painful erections with intervening periods of detumescence, known as "*Stutter Priapism*". The clinician should consider the association of Ischemic Priapism when there is history of illicit drugs (e.g. Alcohol, marijuana and cocaine), anti-hypertensives and/or Trazodone. There may be a prior history of circulatory disease, haematological abnormalities or malignancies. The confirmation of low or absent cavernosal blood flow, with penile Doppler Ultrasonography, will confirm the diagnosis. Cavernosal blood gas testing would support the ischemic state; contrary to Non-ischemic Priapism when the findings are those of arterial blood.

The management of ischemic Priapism is a medical emergency and should be initiated if the condition lasts for more than four hours, starting from the time of onset rather than presentation for medical attention. If the erection lasts for six hours or more it is described as "*fulminant Priapism*". The first line therapy is aspiration of corporal blood, followed by saline irrigation. The patient should be warned at the outset that 1 in 4 cases may end up with some degree of ED; irrespective of conservative or surgical management. The addition of Phenylephrine, a selective alpha adrenergic agonist, to the irrigation solution in a concentration of 100 μg/mL is usually effective. The patient requires continued medical observation for Phenylephrine side-effects (i.e. hypertension, bradycardia, tachycardia and/or cardiac arrhythmia). This requires additional caution in patients suffering cardio-vascular disease. Phenylephrine should not be used in neglected cases lasting for more than few hours; as it can cause ischemia, permanent corporal fibrosis and ED.

Tailoring the dosages for ICI, in the treatment of ED, avoid the complications of Priapism. The clinician must bear in mind that the patient's response to ICI is likely to be better in his own home; due to the clinic associated anxiety. Consequently, the effective dose may be even lower than that which was required to achieve erection initially at the time of dosage titration. The patient should also be advised not to promote erection, beyond functional necessity or an hour of time. He should be warned to exercise (e.g. climbing stairs), if erection lasts for more than an hour, to encourage diversion of blood to the muscular system (i.e. arterial steal phenomenon). He should reduce the subsequent ICI drug dosage.

The general management of sickle cell disease, better fluid, electrolyte and oxygen balance would reduce the chance of Priapism. Otherwise, management should follow the above guidance.

Surgical management is a urological emergency. It should not be delayed, if conservative therapy fails; as Priapism lasting for more than 24 hours can lead to permanent ED. Continued Priapism, lack of improvement in penile regurge, intra-corporal pressure or detumescence are indications for surgical intervention. Surgery aims at shunting the stagnant blood from the corpus spongiosum into superficial venous drainage and bypassing the deep veins. These shunts are usually temporary and close spontaneously following the establishment of normal deep venous drainage. There is a range of urological techniques. The Winter's "Distal Shunt" gained first line status, due to its simplicity and effectiveness. A biopsy needle is used to create fistulae between the glans penis and the corporae cavernosae, under local anaesthesia. If this fails, there are choices of more elaborate "Proximal Shunts" (e.g. Cavernosae-Spongiosum shunt, dorsal vein-cavernosal shunt or saphenous vein bypass).

Long lasting Priapism and failure of conservative and surgical management can lead to chronic fibrosis, oedema, shortening and/or continued partial erection. The management of any subsequent erectile dysfunction should be handled cautiously. Oral treatment could be initiated when the patient recovers and regains confidence. Surgical implants for the treatment of persistent ED should be delayed; as many patients recover gradually and may not require prosthesis.

Non-ischemic, high blood flow Priapism is an arterial phenomenon; resulting from traumatic laceration of the cavernosal artery; leading to excessive blood flow into corporal lacunar spaces and bypassing arterioles. It presents with chronic well tolerated tumescence. There is typically a history of trauma, followed by non-painful constant erection and increased rigidity with sexual stimulation. Perineal Doppler Ultrasonography is useful for identifying the high blood flow. The mainstay of diagnosis is Pudendal arterio-graphy. It will reveal the presence of arterial-lacunar fistula and/or leak at the site of arterial laceration. Selective Embolisation of the lacerated artery is a therapeutic option. Ligation of internal pudendal or cavernosal arteries leads to chronic corporal fibrosis and permanent ED. Non-ischemic Priapism itself does not have a high risk for ED; despite the inconvenience and distress caused by persistent erection. Expectant management is therefore a safer option; compared with the potential risk of selective Embolisation.

Chapter X

Hypo-Active Sexual Desire Disorder, Female Orgasmic Disorders and Hyper-Sexuality

Hypo-active Sexual Desire Disorder (HSDD)

Hypoactive Sexual Desire Disorder (HSSD) is defined as the persistent and/or recurrent absence or deficiency in sexual fantasies and desire for sexual activity. Impaired sexual desire is a common complaint among women presenting at the sexual dysfunction clinic. It is likely that some women lack spontaneous interest in sex but able to respond to their partner's approaches and do not present for clinical care. On the contrary, those who lack interest in initiating sexual activity or averse to their partners sexual approaches, are more likely to present. The patient's presentation for medical assistance is an indication of HSDD associated distress. Surveys indicate that a proportion of women enjoy sexual activity, without reaching orgasm, but do not call for clinical assistance. In these conditions, the clinician should respond to the patients' complaints. Onset (rapid or gradual), duration (lifelong or acquired) and context (situational or global) are basic history points required for the initial assessment. Negative sexual experiences in early life should be explored in women with primary and global impairment of sexual interest; whereas, inter-relationship problems are more relevant in women with secondary or situational impairment of sexual interest and secondary orgasmic disorders.

Female sexual desire requires a fine balance of neuro-endocrine responses. The sex hormones prime the brain to a state of neuro-transmitters that is responsive to sexual stimuli. Oestrogens, testosterone and progesterone are involved in brain receptivity, permission and initiation for sexual activity. There is a requirement for a balance of dopamine, serotonin, nor-epinephrine and other neuro-modulators. Consequently, any disruption of these elements may lead to HSDD.

Impaired sexual desire may be precipitated by depression, whether primary or post-natal. Chronic disease, chemotherapy, antidepressants, antihypertensive, SSRIs, alcohol, recreational drugs (e.g. opiates), low androgens (e.g. oophorectomy) and hypothyroidism are common causes.

Sexual Arousal Disorder in women, without associated impairment in sexual interest, is relatively uncommon. Genital arousal requires fine balance between sex hormones and neurotransmitters. Oestrogens, progesterone and testosterone prime and maintain vulval and vaginal sensitivity, vasocongestion and lubrication; that is necessary for arousal. This is mediated by a balance of neurotransmitters, namely: serotonin, acetylcholine, nor-epinephrine, nitrous oxide and vaso-active intestinal peptide. The most common clinical presentation of sexual desire disorder is usually part of post-menopausal changes. Oestrogen deficiency, leads reduced central and genital responsiveness to sexual stimulation. The associated vulvo-vaginal atrophy, reduced vasocongestion and lubrication aggravate the condition. The There is reduction in arousal associated vulval sensitivity, vaginal swelling and/or lubrication. Treatment should aim first to correct or reverse the suspected underlying cause. Specialised psychological assistance is required when there is relationship and interpersonal issues.

The Female Sexual Function Index (FSFI), Sexual Interest and Desire Inventory (SIDI-F) and Female Sexual Distress Scale are examples of questionnaires that provide an elaborate tool for research situations and therapeutic trials. They measure a specific outcome. They provide objectivity into the process of clinical assessment, effect of counselling and response to therapeutic modalities.

Hypo-active sexual desire in men is relatively a rare presentation on its own; possibly due to an overriding influence of the associated ED. The reduced desire may be secondary to ED. Couples occasionally seek help when there is discordance between the partners' level of sexual interest. Primary sexual interest disorder in males should arouse the clinical suspicion to exclude endocrine conditions (e.g. Hyper-prolactinaemia or Hypogonadism). Secondary impairment of male sexual interest may be the result of depression, disturbed inter-personal relationship or both. The effects of alcohol and/or recreational drugs (e.g. opiates) should not be underestimated. Antidepressants, Anti-lipidaemic, Diuretics, Anti-androgens and/or Antihypertensive are common prescription drugs in middle and later age males. Each group of drugs may lead to reduced desire by direct effect or secondary to ED. The original cause must be reversed first before contemplating additional therapy.

Female Orgasmic Disorders

Female orgasm is an intense feeling of pleasure that follows the stages of sexual arousal and excitement, which is accompanied by involuntary rhythmic contractions of the vaginal sphincter muscles, followed by myotonia and resolution of the sexually induced vaso-congestion. The degree of sexual satisfaction seems to be more important to the interpersonal relationship, as many women report not experiencing orgasm, but are satisfied with their sexual experience; in a personally responsive and unique manner. Women presenting with orgasmic disorders do not usually have problems with arousal. The usual complaint is either marked delay and/or diminished orgasm, following stimulation. The clinician should consider the diagnosis, in relation to what is expected for a woman of a similar age or sexual experience. Women of older age report delay and decline in the intensity and pleasure experience of orgasm; as compared with her earlier years. She will go on to indicate that she requires higher sexual arousal to experience orgasm.

Orgasm could be initiated by imagery stimulation, which depends on perception. It does not constitute a simple reflex response. It is possible that imagery activated orgasm relates to different cerebral centres. Clitorial stimulation and intact sacral reflexes are essential for female orgasm. Women who suffer complete spinal cord injury, above the level of pelvic nerves, continue to experience orgasm following clitoral self stimulation, but not due to vaginal-cervical stimulation.

Orgasmic disorders could be a reflection of psychiatric disorders, interpersonal and marital conflicts, and/or the use of antidepressants. Social cultures and the woman's own religious belief influence her ability of having and enjoying orgasm. Therefore, the management of female orgasmic disorders are challenging; and a multi-disciplinary team approach should be considered.

The clinical history needs to be thorough and exploratory. The clinician should identify whether the problem is a matter of delay or difficulty in reaching orgasm; or the complete inability to achieve orgasm (i.e. *anorgasmia).* Whether it started since coitarch or at a later stage (i.e. *primary or secondary),* gradual or sudden in onset; and whether with any or a specific partner (i.e. *Global or Situational)* should be clearly identified. Drug related anorgasmia may be encountered in patients taking recreational drugs, narcotics, antipsychotics, antidepressants and/or anorexic drugs. Other pelvic and/or sexual dysfunctions may contribution into the woman's orgasmic disorder.

The management should aim to exclude and correct any underlying organic condition which is likely to lead to secondary orgasmic disorders. Vulval Dermatosis, genital and pelvic pain disorders, oestrogen deficiency and post menopausal vulvo-vaginal atrophy and pelvic floor weakness could play an important role in the initiation and exaggeration of orgasmic disorders. The couple may benefit from sex education, to learn about the role of Clitorial, G spot vaginal and cervical stimulation. The "sensate focus programme." is beneficial for interpersonal readjustment. Cognitive behavioural techniques and psychotherapy should also be considered. The role of the woman's pelvic muscle strength in achieving orgasm was first acknowledged by the Chinese. Kegel exercise is beneficial in patients with weak pelvic floor muscles, which is usually a cumulative effect of repeated vaginal child birth; and could be perpetuated by oestrogen deficiency. Review of antipsychotics and antidepressants may reverse the rapid onset orgasmic difficulty; otherwise their side effects may benefit from treatment with Bupropion.

Hyper-Active Sexual Desire Disorder (Hyper-Sexuality)

The definition of hyper-sexuality is challenging. It encompasses excessive sexual activity, namely: sexual fantasies, sexually orientated dreams, increased libido, frequency of spontaneous erections, masturbation and/or sexual intercourse. It becomes clinically significant when either partner complains. Understandably, the assessment is subjective. Decrease in the sexual drive of the partner and pressures in the relationship are contributing factor.

Half of the Parkinson Disease patients report hyper-sexuality following Dopaminargic replacement therapy. It is more notable when the index patient is young and/or male. More female partners complain of their partners' increased demand for sex. Frontal lobe syndrome and dementia, associated with motor neurone disease, similarly produce hyper sexuality. It may express itself in less marked forms of vulgar verbal sexual comments and exhibitionistic behaviour.

Some drugs are associated with hyper-sexuality. Antidepressants may increase sexuality, via improvement in the loss of libido associated with the depressive illness, or centrally via a catecholaminergic effect. Drugs that enhance the catecholaminergic function are associated with hyper- sexuality. Sympathomymetics, Dopaminergic agents, Apomorphine, Amphetamines and/or Cocaine may lead to hyper-sexuality. Testosterone and Anabolic Steroids promote sexual effects that make the patient prone to hyper sexuality.

The Sensate Focus Programme

The Sensate Focus programme aims to allow the couple to experience the feelings of physical contact. It is about one's own pleasure as well as that of the partner, with a clear commitment of not having sexual intercourse. The main goal is to promote a sensual rather than a sexual experience during the period of the exercise. To achieve this, the couple must abandon any attempt of intercourse or genital contact for the initial stages of the programme. The programme may be contrary to the couple's past sexual experience, which was mostly physical and/or genital.

The programme takes 6 stages; the length of each depends on the partners' growing relationship and the speed at which they attain the goal and experience of each stage. Each partner has an equal status in this exercise. Each one has his/her own experience and feelings; and each having an equal responsibility. The partners should set a time for the exercise (e.g. 3 times a week). The three-weekly sessions are divided by 2 parts. Either partner can initiate the session, which would only proceed if the other accepts the invitation. There should be an understanding that the recipient will later interact. In the second part, the recipient undertakes the active part of caressing and touching. Initially, the recipient acts as a spectator, concentrating on relaxation and reading the pleasurable reactions perceived by the active partner. The role is then reversed, when the active partner acts as a recipient and spectator. The exercise requires open talking and communication between the partners to enforce the feelings of pleasure, enjoyment and intimacy. Each partner needs to communicate with the other points of like and dislike and protect oneself against displeasurable contact. Either partner should have the ability to stop if and when s/he feels.

Stage 1 involves the active partner touching the recipient for own pleasure. There are elements of selfishness and exploration. The active partner aims to find areas to touch that produce his/her own pleasures. The recipient is detached from his own pleasurable sensations, relaxed and watchful of the partner's enjoyment on touching and caressing. Neither partner should aim to promotes arousability; to the point of tension, sexual intercourse or orgasm. If the recipient experiences pain or displeasure s/he takes the partner's hand elsewhere. The partners then exchange roles; with the active one playing the role of the recipient.

Stage 2 aims for touching and caressing for mutual pleasure; without genital contact. The recipient guides the active partner into actions that are more pleasurable (e.g. caressing in a slower, faster, harder or softer manner). Each individual aims to enjoy touching and caressing; both as an active participant and a recipient. The partners then exchange roles. The first and second stage helps the couple to realise the sensuality and intimacy they may have lost. It aims to bring the couple physically and emotionally together, in touching each other. It promotes the understanding of sharing, giving and receiving pleasure.

Stage 3 involves genital contact; without caressing or orgasm. Both partners are taking turns in touching the genitalia and being touched. The partners should not allow orgasm to take place, but rather enjoy the experience of touching and being touched. The partners then exchange their roles as active and recipient.

Stage 4 involves genital contact with simultaneous caressing, avoiding intercourse or orgasm. The partners should start this stage when they feel at ease with each other. Arousal may come and go; to encourage a relaxed feeling away from the pressures to perform intercourse.

Stage 5 involves vaginal containment with the erect penis; following achieving the stage of genital contact leading to penile erection. The aim continues to be the sensation of physical contact between the partners. One is playing the active role and the other the recipient; without the frustration of failure to achieve orgasm, or performance anxiety. The woman takes responsibility for insertion; by kneeling above her partner and lowering herself gradually. Disengagement and restarting assures the couple with attainment of purpose. Initially, the partners should allow vaginal containment for a brief interval (e.g. 20 seconds); and gradually increasing the time of containment with experience. The partners should aim to achieve the sensual experience; rather than orgasm. Thrusting should be avoided at this stage.

Stage 6 encompasses vaginal containment with thrusting movements. It starts with touching and caressing, in a pleasurable way for both partners. The goal is receiving and giving pleasure; starting with non-genital caressing, as described before; progressing to genital caressing then arousal and vaginal containment. Both partners may try a thrusting movement for a limited time, initially. Positioning is a matter of choice between the partners and should be open to individual comfort and favour.

The therapist should be comfortable with discussing the details of the programme with the couple. Their confidence in the clinician is of paramount importance. Some couples appreciate written instructions. Others may view the exercise as technical, embarrassing and/or lacking spontaneity. The clinician needs to agree a commitment with the couple; for the six stages and the length of time, which could extend to several months. Feedback helps the clinician and the couple to ensure the application of each stage, reassert its purpose and redirect any diversion. There are benefits of having this feedback after every stage. The program should be adapted to each partners' situation.

Chapter XI

Vaginismus, Sexual Aversion Disorder (SAD) and Sexual Phobias

Vaginismus

Vaginismus is a clinical syndrome involving the involuntary persistent or recurrent difficulties of the woman to allow penile-vaginal intromission, due to anticipating fear and/or experiencing pain; affected by pelvic floor muscle contraction. Penetration related fear of pain is crucial in the development and maintenance of Vaginismus. The condition could be of lifelong nature, since coitarche (i.e. *Primary),* or following a period of previous normal sexual intercourse (i.e. *secondary).* The woman may not tolerate or allow vaginal penetration to any extent (i.e. *total Vaginismus).* The woman would not allow any form of intercourse or any attempt of vaginal examination. A sub-group of women would continue to have intercourse despite the pelvic floor muscle spasms; and may allow some degree of gynaecological vaginal examination (e.g. using a children speculum). The woman would be able to tolerate penile-vaginal penetration; but experience difficulty, stress and pain (i.e. *partial Vaginismus).* Patients' complaints of dyspareunia, Vestibulodynia and/or Vaginismus have wide areas of overlap. The definitions of superficial dyspareunia and Vaginismus are too exclusive or well demarcated. There are patients who present with a mixture of the both conditions; to variable degrees. At its extreme end, non-consummation of marriage, painful or difficult penetration is the presenting symptom. Some patients complain of Vaginismus but describe otherwise satisfactory sexual relationships, in the absence of penetration. They may come to clinical attention only after a difficulty in a gynaecological examination (e.g. cervical cytology tests). Finding the underlying cause is a usually a clinical challenge. The cascade of fear of penetration, anxiety, autonomic sympathetic over activity, lack of vaginal lubrication and defensive contraction of the pelvic floor muscles, will lead to Vaginismus. The ensuing pain, on any attempt of sexual intercourse, will perpetuate a vicious cycle. A small group of women, complaining of Vaginismus, describe a focal past traumatic experience (e.g. gynaecological examination by an unsympathetic clinician or traumatic sexual intercourse with a partner). Child sexual abuse ranks high in the list of causes in medical literature; but is less reported in surveys and clinical situations. On examination, the woman may exhibit body reactions in expression of her pain and anxiety; namely: levator ani spasms, tension of buttocks, contraction of thighs, arching of back, defensive retraction, and ultimately refusal of any form of gynaecological examination. Women who expressed disgust with the idea of penile-vaginal penetration are better considered for Sexual Aversion Disorder and psychotherapy.

The mainstay of diagnosis is the clinical history; supported by examination. As with other genital, pelvic and sex related pain syndromes the *pain diary* is a useful tool, to both patient and clinician, to identify objectively the site, duration, type, extent of pain and response to therapy. The assessment should include sexual and relationship history, the degree of penetration and/or pain and the ability to insert internal tampons or allow any form of pelvic examination (e.g.. cervical cytology). Questions about arousability, climax and sexual satisfaction, help to make the diagnosis and further the management in line with other aggravating factors. The clinician need to identify the degree of anxiety, expression of pain and distress with the proposition of clinical examination; which are central for the diagnosis of Vaginismus. The diagnosis should aim to exclude organic causes; which may be the main or perpetuating aetiology. Infective vulvitis, genital dermatosis, Vulvo-vaginal oestrogen deficiency, hyperactive levator ani muscles, pelvic neuropathic pain, pelvic fibrosis, due to radiotherapy or poor surgical outcome, can cause Vaginismus. The clinician needs to explore the woman's personal issues and past experiences with sensitivity. Issues, like anxiety, depression and/or personality disorders may contribute to Vaginismus. The underlying cause of Vaginismus may relate to inter-relationship problems; namely: personality conflict, abuse, lack of intimacy, inadequate foreplay, inadequate arousal and/or sexual dissatisfaction. There is a wide agreement between clinicians that woman experiencing Vaginismus, more than those who complain of dyspareunia, express negative views about sexuality, exhibit more distress and avoidance behaviours and is more fearful and unwilling to bear any pain. The clinician needs to be perceptive of the range of distress with the gynaecological examination, which may vary from the mere verbal expression of discomfort to the complete refusal of any kind of examination. There is a need for vaginal examination to exclude organic causes; but should not be pursued without the patient's expressed approval and co-operation; as unsympathetic examination is counterproductive.

The management should aim to exclude organic causes as their individual management may well cure or at least alleviate the problem. Some underlying causes may be prominent from the clinical history (e.g. post radiotherapy fibrosis); and others require specific investigations (e.g. pelvic nerve entrapment). Identifying an overlap with other genital or pelvic pain syndromes, in the process of clinical diagnosis and root-cause analysis, would help to direct therapy into radical rather than symptomatic treatments. Nociceptive pain, relates to covert or overt tissue damage; whilst neuropathic pain relates to the experience of perceiving pain, whether the signals are generated in the peripheral nerves or centrally. Nociceptive pain is typically continuous at night whilst neuropathic pain is significantly reduced or absent during sleep. Psychogenic pain, as a response to grieving, should be considered cautiously. Systemic analgesia and *neuro-modulator drugs (e.g. .Amitriptyline, Gabapentin and Pregabalin*) have a place when neuropathic pain is an issue.

The use of *Vaginal Trainers*, commercially known as *vaginal dilators*, is a helpful first line management. The exercise programme helps to promote patient's self-confidence and self reliance; with the knowledge that she is least likely to harm herself. Evidence reports of over 70% success of vaginal trainers. Pelvic floor relaxation, exercise, genital self-contact, massage and awareness could be undertaken as part of the S*ensate Focus Exercise. Physiotherapy, electromyography, biofeedback* are also employed in the management of cases where pelvic floor over activity is not overcome by vaginal trainers and improved patients self-confidence. There are anecdotal case reports of success of *hypnotherapy*. The injection of *botulinum neurotoxin,* to blocks the release of the neuro-muscular transmitters, leads to temporary muscle paralysis in the area injected. The procedure contemplates injection of the pubo-rectalis muscle, in three separate points, on each side; which leads to muscle weakness and subsequent loss of the pelvic floor spasm.

The result appears after several days and remains for some 3-4 months; which may require repetition. Botulinum neurotoxin is not licensed for the management of pelvic floor dysfunction; but there are anecdotal case reports of its successful use. The clinician should aim to overcome the patient's mental block, against penetration, rather than mere muscle paralysis with consequent dependence on repeated muscle blocks. The injection could be part of a pelvic, emotional and relationship rehabilitation programme. The *surgical release of Pudendal Nerve entrapment* provides good results; in the well selected cases.

Psycho-sexual behavioural therapy, to address the patient's negative regard to sexuality (i.e. Fear, disgust, repulsion,…), to improve confidence, self-esteem and image, should be considered as a first-line treatment with primary Vaginismus. It could be considered in parallel with pelvic floor rehabilitation and pharmaco therapy. Personality and affective disorders, extremes of anxiety or depression, require specialised psychotherapy.

Sexual Aversion Disorder (SAD)

Sexual aversion disorder (SAD) is a clinical syndrome where the patient behaves in an involuntary neuro-vegetative pattern with suspicions, phobia, anxiety and distress in response to a sexual stimulus or context. It may be associated with a sense of frustration and/or sexual inadequacy. The term is better reserved for conditions where there is expressed phobia or panic reactions, rather than mere avoidance, of sexual intimacy. The underlying mechanism is a cascade of phobia, anxiety, autonomic–sympathetic over stimulation, increased epinephrine and non-epinephrine release, reduced oestrogen and adrenal androgens. There is a value in interviewing couples with sex related problems separately and together, at some stage during the clinical assessment. There have been cases were SAD became prominent from the partners history; which was concealed initially by the woman. SAD may be *primary*, since coitarche, or *secondary,* following a problem free initial period. Traumatic past sexual experience, during childhood, adolescence or adulthood, have been traced in some cases. Therapeutic procedures that have a high impact on body image were identified in secondary cases (i.e. mastectomy for breast cancer, leading to lymphoedema and exaggerated with chemotherapy). A range of other personal issues may be the leading cause. The women's perception of becoming physically unattractive, her frustration with unfulfilled attempts of sexual intercourse and/or the partner's ED may precipitate or perpetuate SAD. Some patients also suffer from hypoactive sexual desire disorder (HSSD). Genital mutilation and female circumcision surface as an underlying cause when the patient is encountered by a clinician who is sympathetic and empathetic of different cultural issues.

The management of SAD should address any underlying medical aetiology (e.g. corrective surgery for genital mutilation or cosmetic procedures for body image). Systemic desensitisation, senate focus programme and cognitive-behaviour therapy are best adapted to the particular couple's requirement. The clinician should recognise that unsuccessful treatment may perpetuate the patient's sense of frustration and feeling of failure; in addition to the logistic delay in gaining a positive outcome. Psycho-therapy has a role in patients with psychological problem, which could be apparent from the outset; and early referral is necessary.

Sexual Phobias

Sexual phobia is commonly associated with other sexual dysfunctions (e.g. sexual interest or arousal disorder); but rarely may be a problem of its own. The phobia may be *generalised* (e.g. aversion to any form of sexual interaction) or *situational* (e.g. aversion to seminal fluid). The clinician needs to explore whether sexual phobias are related to an earlier traumatic experience (e.g. child sexual abuse or rape). Lines of management generally follow that of SAD; but the clinician should timely consider the expertise of specialist psychotherapy.

Chapter XII

Disease Induced Sexual Dysfunctions

Vascular Disease

Penile erection requires the integrity of the vascular system, namely good arterial inflow, functional corporal sinusoidal tissue, intact venous outflow and normal blood viscosity. The functionality of the vascular system involved in erection requires an intact autonomic nervous system (i.e. sympathetic and parasympathetic nerves). Disruption of any or all of the vasculo-genic and neuro-genic controls may lead to or contribute to impotence.

Systemic atherosclerosis is the most common cause of arterio-genic impotence. The onset of impotence is usually gradual. The patient would have surrogate markers of atherosclerosis (e.g. hypertension, hyper-cholesterolaemia and/or tobacco abuse). There is a possibility that hyper-cholesterolaemia has a direct effect on the function of the small muscles in the corpora cavernosae. Traumatic injury to the perineum and penile arteries; and extensive pelvic surgery, lead to acute onset impotence.

Primary venous insufficiency, leading to erectile dysfunction, is rather rare. The congenital presence of large veins, leading to excessive leakage, will lead to erectile dysfunction, earlier in life. Age related degeneration of the tunica albuginea will result in inadequate compression of the subtunical and emissary veins. There is a postulate that a similar mechanism may lead to impotence in Peyronie's disease. Venous shunts, between the corpora cavernosae and corpus spongiosum may lead to impotence. The shunt could be congenital or acquired. Blunt trauma to the erect penis, surgical procedures or Priapism will lead to a cascade of venous shunts, leakage and impotence. Following priapism, damage to the sinusoidal endothelium and musculature, through ischemic injury and subsequent fibrosis, will lead to impotence.

Autonomic Neuropathy

A) Diabetes Induced Impotence

Diabetes mellitus is the most common cause for autonomic neuropathy; which could also be worsened by concurrent vascular disease, whether diabetes or pathology induced. The prevalence of impotence with diabetes is influenced by the patient's age, the duration and degree of control of diabetes. Prevalence figures, of up to 75%, are quoted in different studies; depending on the demographics of the studied population. Diabetes counts for one third of organic causes of impotence.

The diabetic male patient is three times more likely to develop impotence than the non-diabetic male. Sexual desire disorders, in diabetic men, are most likely due to a negative feedback; as a result of the man's inability to obtain or maintain erection to a satisfactory intercourse. The resultant anxiety, stress, depression, cognitive interferences and relationship conflicts are bound to reduce a man's desire for sex.

Autonomic diabetic neuropathy is the main cause of impotence in diabetic men. Its association with evidence of other pelvic autonomic neuropathy (e.g. bladder and intestinal dysfunction) is significantly higher with diabetic impotent males than potent ones.

Microscopic studies of penile and pelvic autonomic nerves indicate changes in the impotent diabetic patient, but not the non-diabetic one. Ultra-structural changes of penile nerves of impotent diabetic patients are a constant finding in studies; similar to changes in nerves elsewhere. Inducing diabetes, in animal laboratory models, lead to ultra-structural changes in the penile nerves. The corpus cavernosum tissue, obtained from diabetic patients, had a lower content of nor-epinephrine, acetylcholine esterase and VIP. There is also evidence of cholinergic nerve dysfunctions. The longer the duration of diabetes, the less the ability of the cholinergic nerves to synthesise acetylcholine.

The functionality of the smooth muscle of the corpus cavernosum requires intact autonomic nerve mediated relaxation, which is impaired in diabetic patients.

The vasculo-genic changes of diabetes mellitus, leading to arterial wall fibrosis, luminal reduction and impeded blood flow, contribute to impotence. It is perpetuated by atherosclerotic changes, which takes place at a younger age in diabetic patients. Atherosclerosis has a detrimental effect on the cavernosal smooth muscles, which are replaced by connective tissue; and alteration in the fibro-elastic components of the trabeculae. Both lead to veno-occlusive dysfunction. Thus, the elements that are required for the physiology of erection, namely the penile vessels, the cavernous tissue, interstitial tissue and fibro-elastic frame, are all affected in men with diabetes.

The loss of the fibro-elastic frame compromises the ability to expand the trabeculae against the penile tunica albuginea; which compromises the ability to compress the subtunical venules, leading to excessive outflow (i.e. inability to entrap the intra-cavernosal blood, to achieve rigidity and tumescence).

Studies elucidated a primary gonadal dysfunction in diabetic impotent men. They have shown thickened seminiferous tubules, peri-tubular and intra-tubular fibrosis, tubular sclerosis, Leydig Cell dysfunction and increased interstitial collagen.

The testosterone surge, in response to human chorionic gonadotrophins (HCG) is blunted in diabetic men, suggesting Leydig Cell dysfunction. On the other hand, there is no consistent endocrine dysfunctional pattern, in diabetic men. Hypogonadism, thyroid disease, hyper-prolactinaemia may coexist but not to a significant percentage.

B) Diabetes Induced Disorders in Emission and Ejaculation

The process of emission is mediated by the sympathetic nervous system. Ejaculation is dependent on both sympathetic and parasympathetic balances. It is notable that one in three diabetic men experience ejaculatory dysfunction. Diabetic sympathetic neuropathy interferes with seminal emissions, into the posterior urethra; leading to reduced volume of ejaculate. Retrograde ejaculation may also be the result of sympathetic diabetic neuropathy, disrupting the bladder neck closure.

Drugs like Ephedrine Sulphate, Pseudoephedrine, and Imipramine Hydrochloride could be used to treat retrograde ejaculation, which may take up to fourteen days to achieve a result.

C) Diabetes Induced Orgasmic Disorders

Patients and studies rarely report diabetes related orgasmic disorders in men. Women with diabetes are twice as likely to experience sexual dysfunctions as those without. There are reports of disorders in female libido, orgasm, lubrication, arousal and pain. In women, there is higher reporting of orgasmic disorders with diabetes; which may be secondary to other diabetes induced sexual dysfunctions. For example, a woman who is experiencing recurrent vulvo vaginal candidiasis, with badly controlled diabetes, is usually tense, anxious and distressed, due to dyspareunia and cessation of sexual activity. Reduced clitoral sensation with diabetic neuropathy may indirectly lead to anorgasmia.

Endocrine Conditions

Endocrine causes of impotence are uncommon. They contribute to around 1% of ED aetiology. Reaching the underlying endocrine cause for impotence serves two purposes: To identify and treat the underlying endocrine condition and to manage the case of impotence. Whether endocrine investigations should be ordered in every case of impotence will continue to be a topic for debate.

Investigations benefit from the understanding of the hypothalamic-pituitary-gonadal feedback control mechanism; which regulates the secretion of the gonadal hormones. Gonadal hormones in turn have a feedback effect on the secretion of LH and FSH. Testosterone has a primary inhibitory effect on LH secretion. Inhibin, a non-steroidal factor that is secreted by Sertoli cells and FSH maintain a feedback regulation relationship; therefore FSH serves as a sensitive marker of the condition of the gonadal epithelium.

Hyperprolactinaemia inhibits androgen secretion; through a central nervous system direct effect. Hyperprolactinaemia, caused by a tumour or hyperplasia, would cause Hypogonadism; and is easily suspected by a simple measure prolactin level. There is evidence that the gonadal-pituitary feedback mechanism is also disturbed in hyperprolactinaemia. The low testosterone level does not lead to the natural rebound increase in LH. It is notable also that testosterone replacement, in individuals with elevated prolactin levels, does not lead to improvement of libido, which support the view of a direct inhibitory effect of prolactin on the central nervous system. In males, hyper-prolactinaemia leads to ED and reduced spermatogenesis. In females, it leads to disturbed ovarian cycles, amenorrhoea, reduced libido and hirsutism. Anti-psychotic drugs may lead to hyper-prolactinaemia, which underlines the sexual dysfunction side effects in both males and females.

Thyroid hormone imbalance is associated with complaints of sexual dysfunction. Hyperthyroidism is associated with increased serum Oestradiol. There is elevated Oestradiol production and reduced metabolic clearance. Increased Steroid Hormone Binding Globulin (SHBG) leads to increased serum levels of testosterone and Oestradiol. The increased oestrogens levels, in males may to decreased libido and gynaecomastia. There is also a suggestion of a primary Leydig cell failure. Hypothyroidism is associated with decreased testosterone secretion and elevated prolactin levels; which underlines patient's complaints of sexual dysfunction.

Patients with *acromegaly* complain of decreased libido and potency, due to low LH, increased serum prolactin, or both.

Cushing's syndrome is associated with low LH, which leads to secondary testicular dysfunction and consequently decreased libido.

There is a relationship between aging and Hypogonadism, in men. Both plasma protein bound and free testosterone and penile androgen receptors decline progressively with age. The associated rise in Oestradiol and SHBG alters Oestradiol: Testosterone ratio; consequently affecting LH FSH secretions.

Hypothalamic-Pituitary Axis Dysfunction

The increasing use of androgens, as recreational drugs, and Oestrogens, most commonly in the oral contraceptive pill, can lead to misbalance of the hypothalamic-pituitary function. Deficiency in the hypothalamic Gonadotrophine Releasing Hormone (GnRH) will lead to Hypogonadism; with intact pituitary function. LH deficiency, may be an isolated factor or be combined with LH-FSH deficiency. The deficiency may also be part of pan Hypopituitarism. Heroin, Methadone and Marijuana excessive use, as recreational drugs, is associated with lower Testosterone levels, which is most likely testicular and central in origin; due to the absence of the rebound increase in LH.

Hepatic Cirrhosis and Uraemia are associated with decreased libido, impotence and gynaecomastia. The underlying cause is most likely testicular, which is confirmed by its blunted response to exogenous GnRH challenge test.

Hormonal abnormalities, in female sexual dysfunction, are less well studied than the male counterpart. The cyclical nature of female hormones and the intake of exogenous ones (e.g. oral contraceptive pills) present studies with a practical challenge. Research studies have also been interested more in postmenopausal changes which limited their age spectrum. In trials, women who receive both oestrogens and androgens had higher scores of sexual desire, fantasies and arousal; more than women who received oestrogens alone or placebo. There was no change in coital or orgasmic frequency.

The long term consequences of androgen therapy in women are not well studied. Therefore, androgens should not be offered routinely to post-menopausal women, except those who have had surgical menopause (i.e. oophorectomy), due to the loss of ovarian androgens and their precursors.

Parkinson's Disease

Autonomic system dysfunction is part of Parkinson 's disease (PD); but partially underlines male and female sexual dysfunction in PD. The PD associated depression contributes more into dysfunctional sexual drive in females as well as males. Depression also compromises the ability to obtain and maintain erections. Observational studies suggest that motor difficulties (e.g. difficulty turning in bed) play a role in some patients; but not in many others. Compromised relationship readjustment to the new reality of the PD patient's motor difficulties, may put strain on the couple. The physically impaired and increasingly dependent PD patient may not be able to continue, in an active role during the sexual act, therefore will be reliant on the partner's active participation. It is not surprising therefore that reports of sexual dissatisfaction are higher, when the PD patient is male. The contribution of PD motor difficulties in sexual dysfunction in the female patient is disputed. There are complaints of Vaginismus in some PD patients.

Multiple Sclerosis

Multiple sclerosis is a demyelinating disease of CNS white matter; characterised by exacerbations and remissions. It affects people in their second to fourth decade, but rarely appears in the first. One in four patients may experience a progressive disease from the onset. Diagnosis is based on clinical assessment and neuro- imaging studies. The clinical symptoms and signs vary widely. The most distressing are fatigue, gait disturbance and micturition problems. Visual impairment, somato-sensory disturbances, intention tremors, dysarthria and/or trigeminal neuralgia may coexist in variable degrees. Among males, four of each five men report erectile dysfunction. Among females, three of each five women report orgasmic dysfunction. Sexual intercourse decreases in frequency or is absent, in two thirds of men and women affected by MS. Women reported decreased genital sensitivity, diminished libido, difficulty in arousal and anorgasmia. Men report difficulty in obtaining and maintaining erection, ejaculatory and orgasmic dysfunction.

Half of the ambulatory MS men complain of some degree of impotence. Completely impotent males have no lumbar or sacral reflexes or suffer other signs of autonomic dysfunction (e.g.. impaired sweating in the lower body). Damage to the sacral spinal cord, which receives the sensory afferent from the genital area, would lead to loss of erotic sensation and loss of orgasm. There are patients who have intact penile sensitivity; but complain of loss of sensation and loss of orgasm; which suggest a central cerebral mechanism that is damaged. Loss of ejaculation may be due to the loss of the sympathetic control (T10-L3). Severe cases of complete sympathetic dysfunction lead to failure of emission. In partially impaired sympathetic function, there is impairment of bladder neck contraction; leading to retrograde ejaculation. MS patient may experience unusual sexual manifestations. Hyper-sexuality (i.e. increased libido, to the point of disruptive social behaviour), genital allodynia and very rarely Priapism, have rarely been reported.

Sexual dysfunction in MS women is temporary and starts abruptly. The genital sensory problems are worst at the beginning of the MS episode; and then improve rapidly. Loss of libido and difficulty in achieving orgasm are the most commonly complained problems. Long term loss of libido and orgasm may take place in some women. There are reports of MS women having disabling vulval Dysaesthesia and Allodynia; distressing vaginal sensory symptoms, decreased vaginal lubrication and dyspareunia leading to Vaginismus.

Neurological abnormalities, in women and men, contribute to the sexual dysfunction; namely, bladder and bowel dysfunctions, paralysis, spasticity and/or contractures. Depressions, impaired self-image, fear of inadequacy are common problems in MS and may contribute to the sexual dysfunction. Sexual Dysfunction may also be perpetuated by pharmaco- therapy (e.g. Tricyclic-antidepressants, beta-blockers, benzodiazepines and/or anti-cholinergic medications).

The management of the MS patient should consider his/her need as well as that of the partner. The partner of the MS patient is exposed to increasing pressures due to the need to care for the MS patient's physical incapacities (e.g. mobilization, toilet needs....). Addressing sexual dysfunction issues should aim to support both the MS patient and his/her partner. The clinician should investigate issues of sexual dysfunction between other disabilities (e.g. micturition and/or defecation dysfunctions). The availability of different modes of treatment, for the male MS patient should be shared with both partners to give them a range of choices. One treatment may suit a certain period of the patient's journey whilst another could be more suitable during a different episode of the disease.

Epilepsy

Decreased sexual activity (i.e. hypo-sexuality) is the main complaint of patients suffering with epilepsy. Rarely, hyper sexuality, in the form of increased sexual desire and increased frequency of intercourse are one of the manifestations of extended twilight state or status epilepticus. Similar effects resulted after temporal lopectomy. Post-ictal confusional state may also lead to hyper sexuality. Similar manifestations are reported in the inter-ictal state, abrupt control of seizure by surgery or pharmacotherapy.

Alzheimer Disease

The history of sexual disinhibitions is usually given by carers of Alzheimer Disease. Reduced sexual activity is a known, but increased libido and sexual activity were reported.

Dementia

Frontal lobe degeneration and dementia may be associated with hyper sexuality, sexual vulgar comments and exhibitionistic behaviour. Medroxy-progesterone acetate therapy may be used in the management, without adverse side effects.

Bilateral Temporal Dysfunction

CNS conditions like post-encephalitis syndrome (e.g. post-herpetic encephalitis), trauma, anoxia, coagulopathy were reported to lead to bizarre sexual behaviours, in the form of exhibitionism, verbal sexual innuendos, frequent public self-manipulation of genitals and sexual assault of the same or opposite sex.

Stroke

Stroke patients, with lesions affecting the caudate nuclei and basal frontal lesions were reported with hyper-sexuality.

Spinal Cord Injury (SCI)

Victims of spinal cord injury have benefited from the acute phase progressive improvement in the management and rehabilitation. As most of the injuries are traumatic in nature, they are more likely to affect active young men. The sensory-motor impairment leads to dysfunctional erection and ejaculation and failure to achieve orgasm; perpetuated by a negative body image. SCI leads to sympathetic and parasympathetic dysfunction, somatic afferents and efferents disruption and distressed body image. Parasympathetic spinal outflow, from S2-S4 spinal segments, is responsible for erection and reflex erections.

Sympathetic input is responsible for ejaculation and psychogenic erections. The somatic afferents, from the genitals, and efferents to the pelvic floor muscles relate to S2-S4 spinal segments and is responsible for the sensory pleasure feeling and pelvic muscle role in ejaculation.

SCI in women leads to inability to control bladder or bowel functions. The associated apprehension and fear of incontinence during sexual intercourse leads to anxiety and loss of libido. Adductor spasms may interfere with intercourse. Vertebral fractures at or below the L1-L2 levels may be associated with impairment in vaginal lubrication, labial engorgement and clitoral erection.

The acute phase of SCI leads to spinal shock and suppression of spinal reflex activity below the level of injury. Reflex activity returns gradually, with spasticity and hyper-reflexia. The patient may have suffered additional injuries and fractures that interfere with sexual intercourse on their own. Incomplete lesions have a better prognosis, whereas complete lower motor neurone lesions suffer the worst outcome. The majority of SCI patients will be able to achieve erection after a year. Reflexogenic erections are usually brief and insufficient for intercourse. Poor sperm function is notable in patients with SCI. Increased scrotal temperature, chronic disrupted drainage of the seminal tract, impaired immune function, anti-sperm antibodies, were all hypothesized. The infrequency of ejaculation, chronic urinary tract infections and Endocrinopathies may contribute to poor sperm quality.

Schizophrenia

The assessment and management of sexual dysfunction in schizophrenia patients is complex and best managed in conjunction of the psychiatrist, who is familiar with the patient's full mental history and therapeutics. Sexual delusions and somatic hallucinations may be part of Schizophrenia. Persistent psychosis is associated with reduction of libido, sexual activity and satisfaction; in both males and females. Past concepts of management (e.g. hospitalization, concern of sexual exploitation and the belief that sexual relationships may exacerbate the condition) lead to restricted interpersonal relationships.

Depression

The lowered self-esteem, reduced energy, inability to develop intimate relationships and loss of interest, are likely to cause strain on most sexual relationships. Sexual dysfunction affects half of the patients undergoing treatment. Patients undertaking antidepressants and/or psychotherapy, complain of varying degrees of sexual dysfunctions. Two thirds of patients suffering with unipolar or bipolar disorder complain of loss of libido and ED.

Prostatectomy

Radical prostatectomy leads to ED in some 50-80% of patients; as a consequence of damages the erectile neuro-vascular mechanism and neuropraxia. Pre-operative factors, like age, co-morbidities, diabetes, atherosclerosis, hypertension, hyper-cholesterolaemia, cardiovascular disease and/or smoking, influence the post treatment outcome. Men with prostatic cancer that elected for "watchful waiting" do complain of ED; but not to the same extent as those who had prostatectomy.

Radiation therapy is a potential damage to the cavernosal tissue, leading to long-term post-radiotherapy ED in up to 60% of patients. The time of onset may be delayed to one to three years later. Patients who receive external beam radiation complain of gradual and progressive ED. Ionising radiation causes endothelial dysfunction and cavernosal fibrosis.

Nerve sparing radical prostatectomy leads to ED for a period, immediately after the operation due to "neuropraxia" of cavernous nerve. The nerve injury leads to loss of the neuro-regulatory functions of the cavernosal tissue, hypoxia, accumulation of metabolic products, tissue degeneration, and atrophy, loss of elastic and smooth muscle fibres, increased collagen content and fibrosis. At a later stage, venous leakage from the cavernous tissue perpetuates ED.

Patients undergoing post operative recovery programme (i.e. penile retraining) suffer less from ED. Post operative penile rehabilitation, using PDE 5 inhibitors or injection of intra-cavernous Vasoactive agents, may not prevent permanent ED; but rather reduce the time required to recover a degree of erectile function. Preservation of the neurovascular bundle supplying the cavernous tissue is thought to improve the outcome of postoperatively, to some extent.

Cystectomy, like radical prostatectomy, carries a risk to cavernosal nerve damage; and would benefit from nerve sparing procedures. The altered body image associated with urinary diversion may contribute significantly to sexual dysfunction.

Aorto-Iliac Disease and Surgery

Aorto-iliac disease may develop in patients suffering hypertension, atherosclerosis, diabetes mellitus, hyper-lipidaemia and/or smoking. Abdominal aortic aneurysm repair is associated with injury to the superior hypo gastric nerve plexus and hypo gastric arteries. Hypo gastric artery occlusion will lead to different degrees of pelvic ischemia and ED. Nerve sparing procedures, to preserve the autonomic nerves overlying the aorta during surgery and endovascular techniques result in less ED.

Rectal Surgery

Colorectal surgery, involving meso-rectal excision, is associated with ED. It is becoming noticeable that laparoscopic surgery for rectal cancer is tenfold more likely to cause ED. The site of injury may be one of the following: the hypo gastric nerves, the pelvic plexus and cavernosal nerves.

Gynaecological Surgery

The disease conditions that pre-existed the gynaecological surgery (e.g. pelvic organ prolapse, urinary incontinence and endometriosis) lead to sexual dysfunction on their own. Gynaecological surgery to address these conditions will affect the symptoms relating to the disease; and may cause improvement in sexual dysfunction. The extent to which the original condition has caused patient distress and the extent of post-operative relief of that distress is more likely to impact on the patient's general sense of well being and functionality; including sexual function. The improvement in health related quality of life and body image is going to impact positively on the patient's overall sexual interaction.

Improvement in the body image has a major contributing factor. There are patients who expect to be "a new woman" following the procedure; and the gynaecologist must give the patient realist and objective expectations. Patient education, prior to the proposed procedure, mitigates the patient's risks of false expectations, sense of dread to her own well being and/or sense of compromise from the proposed surgical procedure.

Pre-hysterectomy depression is likely to continue into sexual dissatisfaction following the procedure and should be managed proactively. There are Gynaecologists who considered sub-total or supra-cervical hysterectomy more favourably, with the view that the cervix has a part to play in sexual response. There has been no strong evidence to justify this procedure on the bases of improved sexual function. Bilateral salpingo-oophorectomy (BSO), in conjunction with hysterectomy, is more likely to impact on the patient's sexual function due to the initiation of premature menopause.

Comparatives between abdominal versus vaginal hysterectomies did not suggest in favour of one against the other. Abdominal hysterectomy patients are more concerned with the cosmetic nature of the scar and abdominal pain; whilst vaginal hysterectomy patients express relief with correcting a patulous vagina, and/or anterior and/or posterior vaginal wall prolapse. Minimally invasive procedures, such as uterine artery Embolisation, do not interfere with body image. They may be associated with improvement in sexual function, due to the relief from the distress caused by the treated condition (e.g. uterine fibroid).

Similarly, endometrial ablation will provide relief from the distressing uterine bleeding. Tubal sterilisation is likely to influence sexual function in different ways. The relief from fear of unwanted pregnancy improves the woman's sense of well being and sexual function. On the contrary, post sterilisation feeling of regret (e.g. due to a new relationship with a different partner and the desire to have children) may be associated with negative impact on sexual function. The most dramatic effect on female sexual functions are those associated with pelvic exenteration and pelvic clearance procedures (e.g. for cervical cancer). The intended removal of pelvic lymph nodes and connective tissue, as a potential site for cancerous cells, will also lead to the removal of the afferent and efferent autonomic nerves. The effect of the vascularisation is not usually as pronounced; unless radiotherapy is added to the treatment. The effects are exaggerated by the post radio-therapy bladder and rectal inflammation and distress. The psychological effects on body image and the physical effects on pelvic autonomic functions are cumulative and require rehabilitation.

Vulval Surgery

Simple vulvectomy is likely to be followed by change in body image, loss of vulval sensation, introitous constriction and dyspareunia. Radical Vulvectomy, in specialised centres, would benefit from different modalities of skin advancement and grafting procedures. These procedures will resumes vulval skin coverage, but not sensations. Post operative introitous constriction will respond to the gradual use of vaginal dilators. The effects of vulvectomy on the patient's body image need also to be mitigated by re-education, training and sex rehabilitation.

Ablation procedures, like LASER evaporisation for Vulval Intra-epithelial Neoplasia, usually have minimal or no effects, on either body image or sexual functions. The healing process may leave an area of hypo or hyper-aesthesia.

Female Vulval Mutilation and Circumcision

Female circumcision, despite world-wide condemnation and out-law, is still taking place in sub-Saharan and north Africa. There are pockets of back-street practices in some western countries. The assailants usually aim to remove the sex sensitive areas, namely labiae minorae and clitoris. In the type known as Sudanese circumcision, the inner lips of the labiae majorae are skinned and the girl's legs then tied together; to cause labial fusion and make sexual intercourse impossible. The subsequent attempt of coitarche is expectedly going to lead to more physical and psychological damage. The clinician will eventually have to deal with the mutilation, physical and emotional child trauma and abuse; that will extend to adult life. There may be a need for corrective surgery and psychological rehabilitation.

Mastectomy

The negative effects of mastectomy on body image are well recognised. Breast implants, preservation of nipples or tattooing, to imitate the appearance of nipples, are in place to decrease these effects. The clinician should consider any hormone replacement therapy, in the treatment of the ensuing sexual dysfunctions, in the light of the pattern exhibited by hormone sensitive tumour cells.

Penile Surgery

Penile amputation, for the management of cancer, does not only influence the body image, but may render copulation impossible. Inguinal and pelvic lymph-node dissection leads eventually to lymph-oedema, and finally scrotal elephantiasis; which complicates the body image and intercourse. Localised penile amputation or radio-therapy, for the early stage, will preserve sexual function.

End Stage Renal Disease
and Renal Transplant

End stage renal disease is associated with ED. Renal transplant undertaking anastomosis with the internal iliac artery leads to ED in one in ten patients due to reduced cavernosal artery blood flow. Both PDE 5 inhibitors and PGE1 demonstrate efficacy in treating ED in transplant patients.

Chapter XIII

Drug Induced Sexual Dysfunctions

The evidence for drug induced sexual dysfunctions comes principally from patients' reported side effects and clinical trials. The best example is the accidental finding of the side effect of Sildenafil during trials for its use in the treatment of hypertension. The reported drug's side effects, on the specific elements of the sexual response cycle, improved our scientific knowledge on the neuro-genic and vasculo-genic control mechanisms. This knowledge forms the basis of current and future research on therapeutics.

The effect of a drug on sexual function depends on many variables, including: the drug's biological effects, potency, dosage, duration of therapy; and the patient's inherent sensitivity and predisposition to sexual dysfunctions. The different elements of the sexual response cycle function in a self-perpetuating feedback mechanism; to activate and maintain the sexual behaviour until fulfilment.

It depends on the integrity of the central and peripheral neural pathway and vasculature of the sex organs. Interruption of one element of this complex system has a negative feedback effect on the others. For example, a patient suffering from the inability to maintain erection gradually loses interest in sex. He will regain interest with the therapeutic assistance to maintain erection.

The Effect of Drugs on Male Sexual Function

The drugs that influence erection may induce impotence or spontaneous erection, culminating to Priapism. The effect is either produced topically, by the influence of drugs on the trabecular smooth muscles of the corporae cavernosae, or centrally, via action on the autonomic nervous system, spinal cord and/or brain. For clinical and practical applications, it is convenient to examine the iatrogenic effect of drugs on different aspects of the main components of the sexual response cycle (i.e. desire, erection, seminal emission and ejaculation). Drugs affecting one element of the response cycle may influence the others by a cascade effect.

The study of drug influence on sexual functions aims to analyse the potential effects of different agents. It is not meant to be guidance or instructions for therapy.

The account can help to explain the underlying association between drug side effects and patient's sexual dysfunctions. The clinician should consider the patient's medical condition as part of the management plane and act within the relevant national and specialist society guidelines and drug-licensing rules.

Drug Effects on Desire

Central Nervous System (CNS) depressants, including hypnotics, sedatives and tranquilizers, have suppressive effect on libido. Drugs used for insomnia, anxiety, psychosis, depression, analgesia, addiction, hypertension and epilepsy can reduce libido. At small dosages, CNS depressants may suppress social reservations and promote libido. Couples have discovered the practical application of small dosages of CNS depressants (e.g. alcohol in low dosages); to remove social inhibitions and promote sexual coercion. The recent finding of the effect of a moderate amount of alcohol in increasing the testosterone level in women may underline the explanation of this effect. Heroin or Methadone addicts complain of loss of desire and ability to achieve or maintain erection.

Yohimbine, α_2 adrenergic antagonist, enhances sexual drive and had been used for therapeutic purposes, in desire related sexual dysfunctions. Its effects support the discovery of adrenergic receptors' role in sexual desire.

Parkinson disease patients reporting of heightened libido with L-dopa, a catecholamine precursor, prompted attention to the pharmacological effects of drugs on sexual desire. Observations of drug side effects suggest that *Adrenergic Receptors* play an intermediary part on sexual desire. Catecholamine increased synthesis (e.g. L-dopa) or decreased degradation (e.g. by Monoamine Oxidase Inhibitors), is associated with increase in sexual behaviour.

Catecholamine releasing agents (e.g. Amphetamine), or uptake inhibitors (e.g. Cocaine), increase libido and sexual activity; an effect which is captured by the drug users. On the contrary, centrally acting anti-hypertensive agents (e.g. α methyldopa) deplete catecholamine reservoirs and were found to depress libido. There are reports of decreased libido in association with α_1 adrenergic antagonists (e.g. Prazocin), β adrenergic antagonists (e.g. Propranolol) or α_2 adrenergic agonists (e.g. Clonidine).

Similarly, *Dopaminergic Receptors* also play a role in sexual desire; which was observed through their therapeutic side effects. Patients taking dopamine agonists (e.g. Apomorphine or Dopamine), or re-uptake inhibitors (e.g. Bupropion), reported increased libido.

On the contrary, patients taking dopamine antagonists (e.g. Anti-psychotics) report decreased libido. In the past penal and corrective institutions exploited the effects of anti-psychotics as a therapeutic tool, to manage uncontrolled sexual desires in sex offenders.

Drugs may induce change in sexual desire by their surrogate *effects on hormones*. The male sexual desire is dependent on the level of testosterone and Dihydrotestosterone (DHT). Drugs that reduce testosterone levels (e.g. β-blockers, anabolic steroids, fibrates, digoxin, marijuana, alcohol and opiates) decrease sexual desire.

Drugs that inhibit androgen binding (e.g. Anti-androgens, Diuretics and Cimetidine) reduce the level of testosterone and sexual desire. Anti-psychotics induce hyper-prolactinaemia, via their suppressive effect of the dopamine receptor activity; and consequently depress libido. Catecholamine depleting agents also induce a high prolactin level. Cimetidine and Ciproterone acetate suppress sexual desire by their anti-androgenic activity.

Chemo-therapeutics reduce libido through their generalized cyto-toxic effects.

Drug Effects on Erection

Drugs that influence erection may induce impotence or spontaneous erection, culminating to Priapism. The effect is either local, by the influence of drugs on the trabecular smooth muscles of the corporae cavernosae, or central on the autonomic nervous system, spinal cord and/or brain. For example, Antipsychotics (e.g. Chlorpromazine and Pimozide) were reported to have led to Priapism. The same drugs have also been associated with reports of reduced sexual desire and reduced erectile function. Labetalol (β adrenergic antagonist) and Prazocin ($\alpha 1$ adrenergic antagonist), Heparin and Hydralazine were also reported to have caused Priapism in some patients although associated with reduced erectile function in others. The earlier identification of Trazodone improved effects on sexual desire were later dampened by the reports of its association with Priapism. Opiate antagonists (Naloxone and Naltrexone) can produce spontaneous erections.

Part III: Pain Disorders

Chapter XIV

Sexual, Genital and Pelvic Pain Disorders

A) Male Sexual, Genital and Pelvic Pain Conditions

Penoscrotodynia: Localisedand Generalised
Provoked, Unprovoked and Mixed
Primary and Secondary

Testicular Pain Syndrome: Localised and Generalised
Provoked, Unprovoked and Mixed
Primary and Secondary

*Prostatic Pain Syndrome

*Bladder Pain Syndrome

*Urethral Pain Syndrome

*Ejaculatory Pain

*Chronic Pelvic pain Syndrome:

B) Female Sexual, Genital and Pelvic Pain Conditions

*Dyspareunia: Superficial, Deep and Mixed
Localised and Generalised
Primary and Secondary

*Dysmenorrhoea

*Endometriosis Pain

*Vulvodynia: Localised and Generalised
Provoked, Unprovoked and Mixed
Primary and Secondary

*Vaginal Pain Syndrome: Localised and Generalised
Provoked, Unprovoked and Mixed
Primary and Secondary

*Vaginismus: Generalised and Situational
Primary and Secondary

*Urethral Pain Syndrome

*Bladder Pain Syndrome

*Chronic Pelvic Pain Syndrome

Pain is defined as an unpleasant sensory and/or emotional experience, associated with actual or potential tissue damage, or described in terms of such damage. Public and medical experience recognises dissociation between the extent or absence of tissue damage and the patient's sufferings from pain, and the consequent impact on physical, psychological and social well being. The individual's response to pain varies between age groups, sexes, social and cultural backgrounds, physical status and other disease conditions.

The clinicians' inability to measure pain, or frustrations of finding a cause, should not divert the attention from the final aim of addressing the patient's complaint and to alleviate suffering. The British Pain Society scoring systems

(e. g. Pain Rating Scale) provide an objective tool for quantifying pain. It provides an assessment for the patient's own account of pain. The clinician may ask the patient to describe her/his own pain as mild, moderate or severe. Alternatively, s/he could use a scale of severity, from one to ten. The use of a patient based measure for pain provides a good rapport, and fosters trust, between the clinician and the patient. It indicates that the patient's own measure of pain, not the clinicians' perception, is the basis of the clinical interaction. The UK General Medical Council, in its principles of "Good Clinical Care", instructed doctors on the recognition of pain and its management, as one of the criteria for being a "Good Doctor". In other words, ignoring the patient's complaint of pain and/or failing to proactively manage the condition, either by treatment or referral to a specialist unit, is a decline in standard of care, dereliction of duty, departure from responsibility and, therefore, opens the clinician to disciplinary procedures.

Clinicians should recognise pain as a "Clinical Sign", record it and aim to alleviate it; if not able to cure it. The US political campaign, for a "Pain Care Policy Act" with the aim of ascension to a "Pain Bell", provide grounds for practical, political and financial support for chronic pain patients and their carers. It will lend support for research, recognition and management of pain.

Acute pain is a defensive mechanism aimed to protect from tissue damage. On the contrary, chronic pain is a dysfunctional process and abnormal perception of pain (e.g. hyperaesthesia and/or allodynia); which involve the central nervous system.

It has a destructive effect on feelings, emotions, reactions and relationships. The pain could be Nociceptive, when there is stimulation of pain receptors (e.g. due to inflammation); or Neuropathic, when there is a dysfunction in peripheral nerves or CNS that lead to a perception of pain.

Sexual health requires a positive and respectful approach to sexuality and sexual relationships, as well as having pleasurable and safe sexual experience, free of coercion, discrimination and violence. For sexual health to be attained and maintained, the sexual rights of all persons must be respected, protected and fulfilled. In this context, sexual interaction should be pleasurable by both parties, leading into fulfilment and resulting in interpersonal intimacy. Pain can lead to the opposite effects.

The expression of pain in relation to sex would lead to a breakdown in the cycle of sexual enjoyment, personal fulfilment and interpersonal intimacy. The person, who suffers pain, may experience being used, distracted and unfulfilled. The partner may feel guilty, of causing suffering, and experience stress, anxiety and sexual dysfunctions. This has the potential of failure of interpersonal relationships. It may lead to seeking sexual fulfilments elsewhere, multiple relationships, breakdowns and risks of STIs.

The terminology of *sexual, genital and pelvic pain syndromes* indicates the patients' conditions when there is no evidence of malignant, inflammatory, autoimmune and/or degenerative disorder underlying the aetiology. There is no ideal or perfect classification for chronic pain conditions. The pain may involve multiple sites, aetiologies and mechanisms. The term "syndrome" is better preserved for conditions where symptoms and signs are complex and not limited to a defined site or pathology. Some clinicians prefer to describe the chronic pelvic pain syndrome when there is more localisation or being perceived by the patient in three or more sites.

The activities of national and international medical associations and societies studying sexual, pelvic and genital pain disorders are biased towards the female patient. There is occasional and sporadic mention of male conditions. The territorial sub-speciality divide, where both gynaecologists and dermatologists traditionally provided vulval clinics, with no similar arrangement for male patients, perpetuates the problem. This has contributed to delay in recognising many of the equivalent male genital pain disorders. The historical failure to recognise genital/pelvic pain syndromes in males, whether or not associated with sex, is a reflection of lack of awareness, clinical interest, scientific observations, objective assessment and medical recognition; culminating to low reporting and a vicious circle. Successive publications, although scarce, indicate that clinical conditions that cause sexual and genital pain in males are not dissimilar to those of female patients. The clinical understanding of male genital pain disorders, occurring with or without sexual intercourse, will help to inform the management of diseases affecting men. It should provide scientific clues for improving the care of female conditions and inter-partner's relationship.

The pace of improvement in the definitions and terminology of genital pelvic and sexual pain disorders is the culmination of the insistent work of study groups, specialised associations and international societies. More lately, there appears to be dialogue and discussion between these groups which improved and simplified definitions. There will continue to be more refined definitions.

The recent classification of *Vulvodynia* as *generalised*, when it affects the whole vulval area or *localised*, when it affects a part of the vulva, will facilitate communication between clinicians. The additional subdivision of each of these categories into *provoked, non-provoked, sexual and non-sexual* provides better quantification and objective definition. The new classification lacks the historical backing that some of the old definitions and terminology have incurred in public recognition. Patient support groups and public information websites continue to use their old terminology; which represent a practical difficulty. In the interim period, it is necessary therefore to continue to recognise these definitions; until the old nomenclatures and new definition merge. In the new nomenclature, *Vulval Visibilities* could translate into localised, provoked and non-provoked Vulvodynia. The *Burning Vulva Syndrome* will denote generalised or localised, non-provoked Vulvodynia. Many of the vulval pain disorders overlap; and in the absence of identified pathology, *Idiopathic Vulval Pain Disorder,* had been used by some clinicians as a generic term. Common with other clinical conditions, there is no sharp demarcation between subdivisions of Vulvodynia. In its current form, the new classification should recognize weather the Vulvodynia occurred as a primary condition or secondary, following a pain free period.

Vestibulodynia described vulval vestibular pain. It could be provoked, non-provoked, sexual and/or non-sexual. The condition could be *primary*, when the woman experiences pain, since touching the vestibule for the first time (e.g. attempted insertion of tampon, vulval examination and/or intercourse). *Secondary Vestibulodynia* describes the condition following a pain-free period. The finding of more pain nerve endings, in vestibular biopsies of women suffering from Vestibulodynia, provides some aetiological explanation. The increased nerve endings in some women, makes them vulnerable to Vestibulodynia. Genetic, immune, hormonal and epidemiological aetiologies were also theorized. Infectious agents (e.g. Candida or Human Papilloma Virus) were considered in some patients; hence the old name of *"Visibilities"*. This may be a casual rather a causal finding. It is also possible that a decrease in pain threshold is precipitated and/or provoked by inflammation. The rationale of multi-factorial aetiology should underline clinical management. Any concurrent vulval inflammatory process should be identified and treated; in parallel with the management of any remaining vestibular pain.

The Burning Vulva Syndrome has also gained recognition as an identified entity. Patients usually describe the condition as episodes of burning or stinging sensation, in all or part of the vulva. The condition could be provoked (e.g. insertion of tampons, intercourse, examination, self-touch ...) or unprovoked. The distribution of the pain along side neural supply of the vulva (i.e. pudendal, genito-femoral, ilio-hypogastric or ilio-inguinal nerves) led to the postulation of "neuralgia" as an explanation. The relevant nerve distribution may express heightened sensation to touch (i.e. hyperaesthesia).

Some patients have concurrent and similar burning sensation in the mouth; known as *"burning mouth syndrome"*.

The medical community was late to recognise that male patients suffer and complain of similar conditions. *The Male Genital Skin Burning Syndrome* could also be generalised or localized, provoked or unprovoked, localised or generalised. Alternatively, in line with vulval nomenclatures for Vulvodynia, *Peno-Scroto-Dynia (DPSD)* could be used as a generic name to cover all presentations of male genital skin pain of unidentified aetiology.

Dyspareunia continues to define recurrent or persistent pain with, during or after penile-vaginal intercourse. Understandably, the recognition of dyspareunia is encountered when a patient brings the condition to the clinician's attention; due to the associated distress and/or interpersonal difficulties. The identification of its site (i.e. superficial, deep or both), help to analyse the root cause and/or management strategies. Secondary dyspareunia would cease to be a category of its own; when the underlying condition's aetiology is identified (e.g. pelvic inflammatory disease or endometriosis).There will continue to be cases with unidentified aetiology; which could prove challenging to the clinician and frustrating to the patient. There will be overlap with other nomenclatures. For example, superficial dyspareunia could be also described as provoked Vulvodynia.

The female Chronic Pelvic Pain Syndrome is recognised as a separate entity when a woman complains of the persistent and/or recurrent deep pelvic pain and/or dyspareunia that are not associated with otherwise pelvic pathology. *Chronic Pelvic Congestion Syndrome* describes the condition when there is confirmation of the presence of pelvic venous congestion, as the underlying cause. She presents with history of lower abdominal pain and deep dyspareunia. There are patients who have concurrent peripheral Venus tone and/or filling abnormalities; which may underline the aetiology. The pelvic vasodilatation and congestion, associated with intercourse, add to the patient's pelvic pain and dyspareunia;

The *male Chronic Pelvic Pain Syndrome* (CPPS) bears similarities; but takes a different line of explanation. Traditionally, the condition was subdivided as inflammatory or non inflammatory. The CPPS typically presents with pain as the predominant complaint (e.g. pelvic, perineal, lower abdominal, rectal, lower back, retro-pubic, testicular and/or penile tip pain); including ejaculatory pain. Discomfort could be significant to the point of interfering with the quality of life. The patient may complains of urinary and/or obstructive micturition symptoms (e.g. frequency, urgency, nocturia, incomplete emptying of bladder and/or abnormal flow). There are no systemic symptoms, but significant psychological morbidity.

Recently, some urologists prefer to consider Urethral Pain Syndrome, Bladder Pain Syndrome/ Interstitial Cystitis and Chronic Pelvic Pain Syndrome under the umbrella of *"Urological Chronic Pelvic Pain Syndrome";* due to the loss of boundaries between some cases.

Vaginismus is better recognised as a separate entity. The patient complains of persistent difficulty in intromission; which may be precipitated by phobia and could be associated with variable degrees of pelvic floor muscle contractions. Vaginismus has a place in history as a cause of unconsummated marriage. *"Primary Vaginismus"* refers to difficulty since the first attempt of penile-vaginal intercourse. Some patients may also experience difficulty with inserting vaginal tampons or having vaginal/gynaecological examinations. When any form of penetration is impossible, the case is described as *Apareunia.* Variable degrees of intermittent or temporary difficulty with intercourse are also encountered. The extreme of anxiety and/or disgust, at attempted or anticipated sexual intercourse, is described as *"Sexual Aversion Disorder (SAD)".*

Odyn-orgasmia, or painful ejaculation, is dually distressing to the incumbent male. The feeling of pleasure that is associated with orgasm is replaced with pain. It may affect patients suffering from acute or chronic prostatitis, seminal vesiculitis, benign prosthetic hypertrophy (BPH) or those with bladder neck dysfunction, whether spontaneous or due to taking anti-depressants.

Clinical Significance

The clinician needs to recognise the condition in patients with intermittent and/or recurrent symptoms; and not necessarily only those with chronic and/or persistent complaints. Some authorities require some 6-12 months of symptoms prior to identifying the condition. In clinical practice, the clinician needs to respond to patients' distressing symptoms. Practically, the process of excluding underlying pathology, identifying the case as of "unknown aetiology" and keeping a pain diary, would require several weeks, if not months. Some pain conditions are characterised by a clinical entity relating to a defined aetiology (e.g. post-vasectomy scrotal pain or pelvic pain associated with endometriosis). Neurological, skeletal and muscular pain disorders may only relate to the pelvic area (e.g. pelvic neuralgia); and should be considered and excluded in the process of management.

Apart from simple analgesics, embarking on long term pain pharmacotherapy requires timely and judicious decisions. The drugs do have side effects and patients with mild symptoms find the side effects are more troublesome than the condition itself. Many patients also feel satisfied that there is no "serious" underlying pathology and draw assurance from this explanation; with no requirement for further medical intervention. The clinician's role is to explain the finding sympathetically; with possible options of intervention and pharmacotherapy. Unfortunately, many patients would have been dismissed by a previous practitioner with the notion that "nothing was wrong". The patient is then left with the dilemma of pain and no recognition. With this knowledge, the specialist needs to be wary that the patient does not wrongly perceive a repetition of the same scenario. The clinician's provision of an identification and name for the condition enforces recognition and acknowledgement; and assists the patient to learn more about the condition from public information sites.

Chapter XV

Dyspareunia:
The Female and Male
Prospective and Management

History of the Management
of Dyspareunia

The first recorded history of sexual pain appeared in the records of the 13th Pharonic Dynasty, in the early second intermediate period, 1980BC. The Ramesseum Papyri described "A women who has pain in her KNS", probably vulva. In the late nineteenth century, Mr Sims, a renown English Obstetrician described a patient begging for medical help with "intense decapacitating" genital pain that led to the non-consummation of her marriage for a quarter of a century.

The first observational scientific study of sexual behaviour appeared centuries later, in the Kinsey's work. Masters and Johnson produced a second round of observational analytical studies. Between the Archaic records and new history, there was a period of lapse of scientific and clinical observations of pain in relation to sex and sexual behaviour. This was not the case with other studies of human functions.

Vascular, musculo-skeletal, neurological, gastrointestinal and even psychological functions received more attention throughout history, and in different civilisations.

The issue of sexual functions and dysfunctions will continue to be riddled with taboos that hampers and complicate meaningful and representative scientific observational studies. Our understanding of sexual functions and dysfunctions will change with the progress and development of our knowledge and understanding.

The wide and diverse multifactorial influences on sex and pain will provide endless statistical possibilities for scientific studies. The deliberations of the American Psychiatric Association for reclassifying Dyspareunia under mental disorder, in the forthcoming Diagnostic and Scientific Manual of Mental Disorders (DSM V), is a reflection of the growing recognition that genital and/or pelvic pain have mental, sexual and inter-personal consequences.

The most challenging clinical conditions are those where patients have no clear pathology but consequent psychological effects. These cases need to be managed as a clinical condition for both partners, rather than an issue for the index patient only. From a Primary Care prospective, most often there is an underlying demonstrable anatomical or tissue pathology, underlying the aetiology of Dyspareunia and would explain the patient's distress.

This pathology need to be addressed first, to resolve the patient's underlying aetiology, before attempting to resolve the consequent psycho-sexual sequellae.

Any underlying potential organic cause should be excluded first; but should not be a barrier to addressing the patient's complaint, if none is found. Genital, Pelvic and Sexual pain disorders may exist without physical and/or psychological aetiology.

The threshold and expressions of pain varies between individuals, genders and cultures. Western women traditionally suppress their expression of pain in an attempt to handle it at a personal level first before seeking medical advice. Women from the Eastern cultures who live in the West express a lower threshold of pain; with links to social pressures.

Male patients are notoriously late in seeking medical advice, which contribute to delayed presentation and may explain the low reporting of "Genital Pain Syndromes" in men. The application of subjective criteria for measuring the extent of pain and the patient's suffering opens the patient's problem to a host of cultural and personal variables, on the part of the patient and that of the clinician. It would not be clinically wise to address the patient's condition in isolation from other factors.

The Correlations between Sexual Dysfunction and Dyspareunia

The excitation stage of the sexual response cycle involves dominant para-sympathetic autonomic nervous activity. Sympathetic autonomic activity and over charging (e.g. due to fear and/or anxiety) will dominate and overtake the para-sympathetic response and lead to interruption of the sexual response cycle. The classification of Dyspareunia as a sexual dysfunction (DSSM IV) was an endorsement and recognition of the strong clinical correlation between both conditions. The current medico-political atmosphere of heightened interest in the management of pain and the recognition of Dyspareunia as "Pain Disorder" in DSSM V should focus the attention to resolving the patient's main problem: Pain. It will lend political support and financial backup for research in pain and dyspareunia. Diverting the attention from pain to sexual dysfunction and providing symptomatic treatment can mislead the clinical care pathway, by overlooking the root of the problem. Investigating and managing the patient's condition of pain, in line of radical rather than symptomatic treatment, is a better and thorough clinical strategy. Pain does not lead to sexual dysfunction in the index patient only. The partner's feeling of guilt, apprehension of causing pain, empathy and sympathy can lead to stress, fear, anxiety, autonomic sympathetic over activity and consequently sexual dysfunction. Similarly, a non-sympathetic partner is likely to lead to disruption in the sexual harmony between the couples. In its severe form, this can lead to Vaginismus. Hence, Cognitive Behavioural Therapy, which aims to change the avoidance and fear behaviour, proves successful. Female partners of males suffering ED may complain from Dyspareunia and report improvement, after the treatment of the male partner.

Clinical Strategies for Investigating Dyspareunia

Doctors may, mistakenly, consider that their main role end by ruling out organic causes for genital, pelvic and/or sexual pain disorders; without addressing the patients' symptom: pain. There is a risk of a dismissive response, if the doctor can not identify a stark underlying cause for pain. This strategy approach misleads the clinician and frustrates the patient. An organic cause for Dyspareunia may exist, but may not be identified by the first line of clinical assessment. Secondly, dismissing the case, as of no organic cause, misses the opportunity of thorough investigations. It hampers the systematic approach to clinical management and wastes the opportunity of identifying the underlying cause accurately, timely and objectively. This makes the diagnosis of "Chronic Pelvic Pain Syndrome" in women or men challenging, and excluding organic causes first. A practical example would be the indiscriminate use of analgesics before excluding pregnancy, pelvic inflammation and/or malignancy.

The remit of investigations is wide and should not replace clinical experience. Investigations should support and complement the process and art of diagnosis. It takes a thorough clinical assessment to select and direct the necessary investigations; and avoid the unnecessary ones. The clinician should pursue an active and deliberate clinical interest and to avoid unnecessary tests.

Listening to patients who complain of pain is of paramount importance. Patients live through their own condition and experience it for longer than the time doctors spend in addressing the problem. Patients often have important information that the physician needs to ascertain. Listening introduces the physician to the patient as a caring and interested doctor, who took her/his problem seriously and proactively.

Taking the patient's own history, as an element of clinical assessment, carries more relevance in the management of pain, than other clinical fields. It will direct the physician's own process of clinical and laboratory investigations in the right direction for identifying the actual aetiology and providing radical rather than symptomatic treatment. Deep Dyspareunia, lower abdominal and deep pelvic pain, can point out to pelvic condition (e.g. Pelvic Inflammatory Disease (PID) in females, or prostatitis in males). Similarly, a history of Superficial Dyspareunia is suggestive of vulvitis, vaginitis or Balano-posthitis. The clinical history of a concomitant condition in the sexual partner (e.g. herpes genitalis or vulvo-vaginal candidiasis), may give a clue for the likely cause. The duration of pain is helpful in identifying its acute, sub-acute and chronic course. Most patients are capable of identifying the difference between burning and soreness, which can put the clinical investigation into a different prospective.

Listening to patients lead the clinical community to recognise conditions that she did not describe before. Dysaesthetic Peno-Scroto-Dynia (DPSD) describes genital pain without an underlying clear organic cause; as the male equivalent of Dysaesthetic Vulvodynia. The condition could be classified as

Generalised or Localised, Provoked and/or Non Provoked. This classification keeps in line with that of Vulvodynia, objective, simple and objective.

History of past treatments could be helpful in identifying what the condition may or may not have been; but should be assessed with some caution. The course, dosage and/or duration of treatment may not have been adequate, with misleading conclusions. For example, it is not uncommon that an episode of a short course of topical anti-fungal treatment is prescribed for what would have been a flare-up, or acute on top of chronic, Vulvo-Vaginal Candidiasis (VVC).

The failure to achieve cure in this case is due to the inadequate duration of treatment rather than wrong diagnosis or choice of therapy. Similarly, a patient with acute episode of VVC on top of an underlying Lichen Sclerosis (LS) may not benefit permanently. Therefore, the clinical policy of assessing the patient's condition, with examination, following the resolution of the acute phase, proves to be fruitful clinically. The use of topical preparations that contain steroids may mask, distort or conceal an underlying pathology (e.g. VVC on top of LS).

The wrong use of steroids during an episode of Herpetic Vulvitis can lead to exacerbation. An interim interval of no topical steroid application is therefore necessary for making a precise clinical assessment for genital skin conditions. History of related other symptoms and/or conditions is necessary to complete the clinical picture and help the diagnosis. Generalised skin conditions also affect genital skin; and vice versa, genital skin conditions may express concurrent stigmata elsewhere. Rarely, what is thought widely to be a generalised disease condition may express itself only on genital skin (e.g. Lichen planus or Psoriasis).

Inspection as a method of clinical investigations has benefited from the availability of magnification, good lighting and recording (Vulvoscopy, laparoscopy and photography). This is another area where investigating male patients has not exploited the available technology. The use of magnification and proper lighting may reveal a lesion that could otherwise be missed by the naked eye examination (sub-clinical herpetic lesions). Vulvoscopy has become a routine and widespread investigation for women presenting with genital dermatological conditions. The use of peniscopy for male genital skin conditions is still scarce, despite the clinical benefits. The use of laparoscopy is also hampered by its practice as a routine, cold procedure, rather than its application in acute conditions (e.g. suspected PID). Photographic records, whether paper, electronic and/or digital, carry an educational value for the clinician and trainees.

It helps to document the patient's own progress. It has proved useful at occasions where there is discrepancy between the patient's own progress and his/her appreciation (e.g. when there was a clinical improvement, with no parallel symptomatic relief).

In these conditions, the patient viewing an identifiable improvement helps her/him to feel positive and encouraged to pursue the management course further. Similarly, where there continues to be a clinical signs but no parallel symptoms (e.g. active LS); the photographic sequence of pathological changes help the patient to appreciate the need for continuing with the treatment.

Examination may give the first clues for the provisional diagnosis and/or direct a well-informed investigation process. Many clinical conditions that cause dyspareunia are identifiable on clinical examination (herpes genitalis, Vulvo-Vaginal Candidiasis and Balano-posthitis). A retro-verted-flexed uterus may entrap the ovaries into the pouch of Douglas; resulting in deep Dyspareunia, and could be identified first by a thorough pelvic examination. It is not possible to overemphasise the importance of patient's contribution and co-operation during clinical examination. Most physicians appreciate the value of a relaxed co-operative patient during vaginal, pelvic and abdominal examination. This poses a challenge on the clinician to gain the patient's trust. Patient's lack of relaxation could be a reflection of anxiety, inflammatory condition.

Abdominal tenderness, rigidity and guarding tenderness contribute into making the diagnosis of PID; and will be supported by the pelvic findings of adenexal tenderness and/or cervical excitation (i.e. pain on manipulating the cervix). Asking the patient to point out the area of pain (i.e. finger pointing test), contributes into making the diagnosis of Vestibulities. A male patient's own retraction of perpetual skin can help in identifying underlying lesions. It avoids undue pain that could result from the doctor's attempt. It can help the patient who may have never retracted his own perpetual skin. The procedure will boost the patient's confidence in retracting his own preputial skin, for self-care and examination, which is unthinkable by some.

Investigations do not only help to support the making of a clinical diagnosis but may also help to exclude another. In a litigious and medico-legal culture, there is a place for supportive laboratory evidence, to corroborate the clinical findings. Microbiological investigations are necessary to confirm or exclude the offending organism/s in genital and/or pelvic inflammatory conditions. Negative microbiological investigations do not necessarily mean the absence of inflammation, as the underlying cause of pain (e.g. PID with negative microbiological tests).

Lower abdominal, pelvic, urinary tract and testicular ultra-sonography is a non-invasive but widely available and helpful investigation. The availability of trans-rectal and trans-vaginal probes and the recent high-resolution ultrasonography have made the investigation practical and valuable in daily practice. C Reactive Protein (CRP) and Erythrocyte Sedimentation Rate (ESR) are supportive in identifying or refuting an underlying inflammatory process. Cystoscopy may help to guide the diagnosis of interstitial cystitis, where the presenting symptom may be dyspareunia rather than micturition problems. There could be a place for allergy testing in some cases of suspected or identified allergic Vulvitis or Balano-posthitis. Practically, the battery of tests is so wide; that an observant patient and a "Pain Diary" are irreplaceable in supporting the diagnosis or narrowing the spectrum of "Allergy Patch Tests".

There is a common strategic clinical failure in the concept of "symptomatic" rather than "radical" therapy, in the management of genital, pelvic and/or sexual pain disorders.

When the patient's symptoms are addressed before the prior systematic investigation and analysis of the actual underlying aetiology, the diagnosis is delayed, if not lost. The strategy of Symptomatic Therapy can miss the opportunity of identifying the cause and perpetuate the underlying disease condition.

The objective assessment of correlation, between sexual function and Dyspareunia, could be achieved by The Female Sexual Function Index (FSFI) and the Female Sexual Distress Scale (FSDS). The questionnaires are time consuming and not practical for a busy clinical setting. They may be given to the patient to fill at home, prior to the clinical appointment.

As self administered questionnaires, they provide an objective measurement of the extent of correlation between the two conditions. The assessment could be replicated in the patient's own case, after a course of treatment, to indicate any future progress and improvement of condition, or lack of it. The scales provide a useful method of communication between clinicians and an objective measure of the patient's condition in comparative studies.

The identification of dyspareunia as superficial and/or deep continues to provide a practical platform for the clinical analysis and reasoning for investigations and treatment. Female and male *Dysaesthetic Superficial Dyspareunia* and *Chronic Pelvic pain Syndrome* should only be reached following a thorough and exhaustive assessment to exclude other underlying pathology that may explain the patient's condition.

Clinical Review of Common Causes of Female and Male Dyspareunia

I) Superficial Dyspareunia

A) Genital Trauma

Genital trauma and its consequences may cause dyspareunia for both females and males. The raphe of the glans penis and posterior midline area of the vulval vestibule are weak points and naturally vulnerable to trauma, during forceful sexual intercourse. The anatomy, delicate nature and positioning of the two areas at the point of thrust and skin stretching during intercourse, make them vulnerable. Trauma to the penile glans' raphe or vulval vestibule is associated with acute severe pain at the point of its first occurrence. Recurrent and sub acute episodes of pain, may be encountered, on consequent attempts of intercourse. The condition is a common complaint in clinical practice, despite the scarcity of medical literature. Sexual intromission, against a contracted pelvic floor muscles, associated with lack of vulval, vestibular or vaginal lubrication can lead to excessive stretch on the penile frenular and/or vulval vestibular skin, leading to tear/s. This initiates a cycle of acute skin tear, followed by fibrosis and loss of skin elasticity, increased vulnerability to stretch, leading to further tears, in a vicious circle.

The lack of vaginal lubrication is a common cause of superficial dyspareunia. Genital skin tears are perpetuated by lack of lubrication and a discordant sexual excitation cycle between the couples and/or bad sexual techniques. An inpatient male, an unresponsive female, or a combination of both, can lead to lack of lubrication and dryness with more pressure and stretch on the genital skin. This is one area where sex education and counselling could provide rewarding results to the couples and the clinician. Avoiding the predisposing factors, by giving time and chance for the natural sexual excitation cycle, and consequently relaxation and lubrication, should be the first resort of medical advice, to avoid the problem. In case of old and fibrosed glans raphe, wearing a condom can give a degree of protection to the skin against further stretching and recurrent traumas. For females, the use of vaginal lubricant creams proves helpful. Manual assistance, from either partner, will help to achieve intromission and avoid undue stretch on vulval or glans skin. If this proves to be unsuccessful and the condition is recurrent, the last resort is frenulectomy for the male.

Inadequate foreplay can contribute into imbalance between the sexual response cycles of the male and female partners. The male may achieve erection before the female reaches the physiological equivalent (i.e. vaginal congestions, transudation, lubrication and secretions from the Bartholin's glands). Assessment and counselling is usually enough to identify the condition and lay the grounds for management. There are benefits of counselling both partners together, to help them acknowledge the problem and reach a mutual resolution. The clinician need to reiterate the value of intimacy. The couple need to explore their feeling and reactions and keep in sexual response harmony. The Sensate Focus Exercise (SFE)] re-programmes the couple into recognising each other's needs, likes and dislikes. The exercise aims to retrain the couple to be aware, respond, react and interact with each other's sensual body spots. It helps to identify what is pleasurable and what is not, in touching each other, short of sexual intercourse. It rebuilds up the physical relationship between the couple from the beginning and emulates gradual and progressive courting.

Genital Dermatosis can lead to skin vulnerability to trauma. Female and male genital skin trauma could be a consequence and first indication of an underlying dermatological process. The skin fibrosis thinning and loss of elasticity that is caused by Lichen sclerosis (LS), can lead to skin vulnerability, in both male and females. LS can lead to skin splitting, infection, inflammation and further scarring; any of which could be associated with pain and dyspareunia. Postmenopausal oestrogen deficiency can cause vaginal dryness and vulnerability to skin trauma.

Atrophic Vulvo-Vaginitis, on their own, can cause dyspareunia or contribute to vulval and/or vaginal skin trauma. Hormone replacement therapy and/or use of topical vaginal oestrogens have improved what was common complaint.

Perineal, Vulval and/or Vaginal trauma during delivery and its consequences measured high in postnatal dyspareunia and sexual disharmony. The psychological effect sometimes outweighs the physical trauma. A traumatic birth, even without genital injury, may lead the woman to lose the desire to have sexual intercourse, feeling that the consequences of sex are pregnancy and rehearsal of the traumatic delivery experience. Prophylactic measures, to avoid and/or minimise perineal injuries, and the appropriate management of tears and episiotomies, have reduced complaints of post natal lack of desire and/or dyspareunia. This does not preclude the physician from proactively excluding the condition; and dealing with it when it arises.

A marked *disproportion* between vaginal and penile size can cause dyspareunia, especially with partners' unrealistic expectations at the outset of the sexual relationship. This should not preclude a successful relationship between the couple; as the vagina is adaptable and amenable to expansion, with practice. The patient's gradual self application of increasing sizes of vaginal dilators could help the process of vaginal adaptation. Identifying and correcting the disproportion and/or obstruction causes of dyspareunia is rewarding, for both the patient and physician.

The *hymen* is usually elastic and would allow sexual intercourse in most circumstances. Rarely a tight membrane may interfere with copulation and lead to Dyspareunia. Self application of vaginal dilators may prove useful. The patient's self insertion of her own finger can boost her own trust in the procedure. Alternatively, operative incision or removal of the hymen could be the last resort; if vaginal dilators fail.

Vaginal Agenesis is rare but may present first with Dyspareunia. Self application of vaginal dilators is efficient first-line management and provide satisfactory outcome. It replaced the previously adopted complicated and invasive surgical vaginal reconstruction techniques.

Testicular Trauma is a common cause of testicular pain. The patient may have experienced a covert mild trauma, forgotten all about it and ended up with an enduring testicular pain. The investigations of testicular pain should proactively exclude STIs and tumours; especially in young men. The genito-urinary clinic may be the young man's only medical exposure. The clinician should provide a through assessment, to exclude STIs and testicular tumours, before reaching the conclusion that the pain may be due to trauma, even in the presence of a positive history of trauma.

Testicular torsion should be on the list of differential diagnosis for Epididymo-Orchitis, as a cause of Dyspareunia. The condition requires a high degree of clinical suspicions; as delay in treatment can lead to arterial constriction, gangrene and necrosis. It requires surgical emergency. Testicular torsion is more common in adolescents. More young men are starting their sexual debut early in life, and experimenting with different positions during sexual intercourse, which contributes to the opportunity of testicular torsion. Ultra-sonography and arterial flow Doppler investigations are proving helpful in supporting the clinical diagnosis. Timely testicular/scrotal surgical exploration, correction and fixation could avoid testicular necrosis and atrophy; with the consequent physical and emotional trauma. Replacement of an atrophic testicle with a testicular prostheses and psychological support is needed, in case of the unfortunate findings of necrosis.

Penile fracture is associated with intense and acute pain during and after the incident. The patient's history leads the diagnosis. There is usually a history of the "partner falling on the erect penis", leading to its fracture. The excruciating pain, associated with intense bleeding and remarkable bruises and haematomas, alarms the patient to seek immediate medical attention. Severe penile fractures are overt. Covert, partial, and mild cases do occur; but still require urgent management. The clinician should be weary of possibility of concealment of history due to feeling of embarrassment. The surgical correction may be followed-up with a degree of fibrosis and distortion leading to sub-acute and chronic Dyspareunia.

Genital *piercing* and *foreign bodies* may cause Dyspareunia in the incumbent patient and/or the partner. The personality and sexual behaviour of individuals undertaking body piercing is suggestive of a desire of uniqueness, self-identity and sexual expression. The practice is intended to increase sexual stimulation and pleasure. It is reportedly more common with homo and bisexuals, with multiple sexual partnerships. Clinical experience suggests that the majority of cases do not suffer Dyspareunia.

Female genital *mutilation* and *circumcision* could be a cause of dyspareunia. Clinicians in western societies need to be aware of its rare presentation; especially in patients with the relevant cultural background. There are cases where the mutilations have taken place in the western country, under the influence of the family matriarch. At its extreme, it may be impossible for the couple to achieve sexual intercourse. It can lead to variable degrees of dyspareunia, depending on the extent of psychological and physical damage. The management of the conditions may require plastic reconstruction for the woman's genitalia, psychological therapy and personality build up for her own well-being and psychosexual counselling for the couple. Health education, cultural reprogramming and legislation are widely adopted in both western countries and home land societies adopting female circumcision.

Male self inflected insertion of a *urethral foreign body*, could be encountered in cases of psychiatric disorders, intoxication and erotic stimulation. There are rare reports of accidents, with consequent pain in the index case and/or partner. The unusual presentation and lack of clear history represent a clinical challenge. A degree of clinical suspicion, supported by radiological investigations, should resolve the clinical dilemma.

Penile *strangulation*, caused by restricting devices, may follow the application of various non-metallic and metallic objects on the penis, to increase sexual performance and erotic gratifications. The treatment of impotence with suction pumps involves the release of a rubber ring over the penile base, to induce strangulation and block blood drainage, which is associated with some degree of pain. Its long term use can lead to lymph oedema, fibrosis and chronic pain.

Post Vasectomy Pain Syndrome is the persistent and/or recurrent testicular pain, following the surgical procedure; and is not explained by another concurrent pathology. Retrograde retention of testicular secretions contributes to the aetiology; but does not entirely explain the condition as many patients do not seem to complain. Pre-operative counselling and informed consent are preliminary procedures and may avoid un-necessary complaints.

B) Psychological Trauma

Sexual abuse leads to physical and psychological trauma and is associated with chronic pelvic pain and Dyspareunia. Female and male patients exposed to child sexual abuse may present with interpersonal malfunctioning, relationship avoidance, high-risk sexual behaviour and variable degrees of sexual dysfunction, including Dyspareunia. Early childhood sexual interference can lead to the woman's inability to have sexual intercourse.

Vaginismus may also be a natural and expected consequence of enforced male behaviour; concurrent with the woman's distress or pain (e.g. Visibilities). The exploration of these cases is challenging, when there is self denial or even no memory for the events.

C) Genital Dermatosis

Loss of vulval skin elasticity and introital narrowing, due to Lichen sclerosis (LS) may cause Dyspareunia for women. The recurrent fibrosis, following repeated traumas and/or infections, may lead to tight prepuce and dyspareunia. The skin damage that affects the vulva can range from atrophy, fibrosis loss of elasticity, recurrent episodes of skin fissures and consequent infection. The cycle will progress with inflammation, fibrosis, and more loss of skin elasticity; with more vulnerability to skin trauma and fissures. In late cases, the vulval skin architecture is lost. The vulval anatomy is reduced into a sheet of atrophic sclerotic skin with no character or labial folds; but constricted vaginal and/or urethral introitous. The clinical diagnosis of Lichen Sclerosis should be suspected on history and examination. The clinical diagnosis of LS should be supported by histological confirmation. LS have a long and recurrent course, and pre-malignant potential.

Traditionally, LS is thought to affect female patients more than males. In males, the condition is known as Balanitis Xerotica Obliterans (BXO) and may be associated with different levels of pain. A fibrous constriction band around the prepuce, lead to hour-glass shape constriction ring that is difficult to dilate; especially during erection. This may be the earliest sign of BXO. Forcible dilatation can lead to skin tears, infection, fibrosis, more constriction and pain. The recent finding of up to 40%, of histological confirmation of BXO on circumcision samples; for the management of Phimosis in young boys, suggests that the diagnosis in males is clinically overlooked and underestimated. This contributes to the biased perception of the differential incidence of LS between females and males. Lichen sclerosis is thought to be more common in children with Acquired Phimosis (60%) as compared to Congenital Phimosis (30%). Understandably, many of these patients will be missed during childhood and may present later with Dyspareunia, due to tight preputial skin that interferes with the natural retraction during erection. Topical treatment with steroidal preparations requires intensive personal care and caries the possibility of complications.

Lichen planus on its own does not usually lead to Dyspareunia; as the condition is mild in most cases. The rare *ulcerative LP* predisposes to secondary infections and severe inflammations in the vulva and vagina, leading to Dyspareunia. The patient's first presentation with acute and severe Vulvo-Vaginitis delays the identification of the underlying ulcerative lesions of LP. Improvement takes place after the initiation of a broad-spectrum antibiotic treatment, for the acute vulvo-vaginitis. Later recurrences occur, within a short period and frustrate the incumbent patient. It is clinically prudent to examine the patient after improvement of the acute inflammation, which may reveal the underlying multiple superficial vulval and/or vaginal ulcerations. The association of vulval ulcers with oral lesions should increase the degree of clinical suspicion and help the diagnosis. Erosive LP is rare, but poses a diagnostic challenge to the clinician; who should review the patient's condition, with examination and through inspection, including Vulvoscopy, during an active episode of acute inflammation, when there is evidence of active erosions. The clinical identification of LP will need a confirmatory punch biopsy under local anaesthesia. Extensive vulval lesions due to LP, its consequent dermatological changes and/or topical therapy could all be associated with Dyspareunia. Skin atrophy, breakdown, fibrosis and cicatrisation are associated with pain and chronic Dyspareunia. Superimposed attacks of skin cracks, tears, secondary infections and inflammation will lead to acute and sub-acute Dyspareunia. The excessive use, or patients' heightened response, to topical steroids can lead to genital skin atrophy, breakdown, secondary infections and Dyspareunia.

The most important aspect of clinical care for LS/BXO is the need for a long-term follow-up programme. The clinical follow up aims to identify complications of the disease and/or treatment as early as possible. It is thought that some 5% of the patients may develop pre-cancerous conditions; which requires early identification. This is possible through regular and planned clinical follow-up. The amount and frequency of the topical steroids also need to be re-adjusted, according to the LS activity. During active episodes, the patient needs to apply the topical steroids more often than during periods of LS quiescence The male preputial constriction ring is amenable to correction by simple multiple vertical incisions, over the preputial constriction ring. The incisions are then sutured transversely (i.e. Preputio-plasty). The incisions should cut through the fibrous ring to allow for more skin slack. The introduction of non-steroidal preparations for the treatment helps to avoid Steroid associated skin atrophy and its consequences, in patients who are vulnerable to topical steroidal complications.

Erosive skin conditions (e.g. Erosive LP) cause dyspareunia on their own; or due to complication with superimposed pyogenic infections. Examination after the cessation of a superimposed acute inflammatory condition (e.g. Candidiasis) is essential to establish or refute an underlying pathology (e.g. underlying LS).

D) Genital Inflammation

Inflammatory genital conditions, including Sexually Transmitted Infections (STIs) are common causes for Dyspareunia. The clinician should be aware that pain may be a way of expressing the underlying anxiety with STIs. The clinician should consider the need to excluding STIs; to provide assurance to the patient and basis for further management. The patient's medical history guides the necessary investigations.

Herpes Genitalis may cause pain, with or without intercourse. The HSV genital lesions were primarily due to Type II (HSV II) infection. The increasing practice of oral sex has led to HSV Type I overtaking in prevalence. A sub-clinical herpetic lesion, that is not easy to identify with the naked eye, may be a source of severe pain and active contagious transmission. The use of

Vulvoscopy and Peniscopy, in these cases, serves to identify the clinical lesion and the best site for swabs and sampling. It is possible to make an accurate provisional clinical diagnosis in over 90% of cases. The value of Polymerase Chain Reaction (PCR) and Nucleic Acid Amplification Techniques (NAATs) in identifying the organism could speed the process of microbiological confirmation of a clinical suspicion. The treatment though, should start on clinical grounds and empirical basis; otherwise, the patient would suffer unnecessarily, until virological confirmation. Superimposed secondary infection may worsen the patient's condition during the attack; adding to pain and Dyspareunia. Most lesions recover with very little or no genital skin damage; but the psychological effects are significant to the patient and the partner. Bilateral vulval or opposing preputial and glans herpetic lesions (i.e. kissing ulcers) that presented lately and/or badly managed, may lead to adhesions, and Dyspareunia. The ulcers should be separated manually and with the help of antiseptic cream or ointment on regular daily basis.

Candidal Vulvo-Vaginitis and *Balano-posthitis* are common causes of Dyspareunia. The pattern of recurrence and lack of effective preventive therapy is frustrating to both patients, and clinicians. Most cases are diagnosed clinically. In clinical conditions that are calcitrant to pharmaco-therapy, fungal culture and sensitivity tests are necessary to inform appropriate treatment. The clinician must consider the possibility of superimposed Candidal infection during the use of the broad spectrum antibiotics. Episodic treatment is effective in most cases, but the route of the problem and predisposing factors must be addressed, to avoid or minimise recurrences. Attention to genital hygiene and skin care, reducing exposure to humidity and temperature entrapment, will provide unfavourable conditions for fungal growth. The patient's condition must be reviewed after recovery, to exclude any underlying lesion that is masked by the inflammatory process; but predispose to its recurrences (e.g. Lichen sclerosis).

Pyogenic genital infections are becoming rare in western countries. Severe post menopausal *"Atrophic Vulvo Vaginitis"* may be complicated by secondary infections. Empirical wide spectrum antibiotic therapy is usually necessary to commence at the point of clinical presentation and prior to obtaining microbiological culture and sensitivity tests. These tests are routinely requested but scarcely lead to a change of the initial therapy. The long-term use of topical vaginal oestrogen cream, on weekly basis, should be considered to support vulval and vaginal oestroganization. Topical oestrogen may be needed, even if the patient is already on systemic Hormone Replacement Therapy (HRT).

Orchitis is presenting less often than it used to be some years ago; most likely due to the liberal use of microbiological investigations and antibiotic therapy for urethritis. The condition of Orchitis is serious enough to warrant immediate attention; effective antibiotic therapy, testicular suspension, and/or hospitalisation. *Apareunia* is the norm, as the pain is severe enough to dissipate any desire for sex. Sexual intercourse would be attempted only in the mildest of inflammatory cases; when the patient experiences Dyspareunia.

Bacterial vaginosis (BV) is not an inflammatory condition as such; but becoming one of the most diagnosed conditions in western genito-urinary medicine clinics. Either or both partners identify the post-coital offensive smell as "fishy odour". The smell is troublesome for the male partner and embarrassing for the woman.

The pain experienced by female patients is usually described as irritation and soreness. The consequences are disharmony, repulsion, distress and apprehension. The couple eventually experience frustration; due to recurrences and lack of preventive measures. The Amsel's criteria (i.e. offensive discharge, high vaginal PH, fishy odour on addition of KOH to a slide containing a sample of vaginal discharge and/or the presence of "Clue Cells" on microscopy of a Gram-stained slide) are useful bedside diagnostic tests. The grading of "Clue Cells" on microscopy of a Gram stained slide, may be used on its own for making a diagnostic criteria (i.e. Nugent method). The treatment of BV with oral Metronidazole is effective; but recurrences are common. Clindamycin vaginal applications are preferable during pregnancy. The use of condoms by the male partner may decrease recurrences; due to less interference with the vaginal acidic PH, by the alkaline semen.

Trichomoniasis is notorious of causing irritation and burning sensation during sexual intercourse. Microscopic examination of a slide containing a sample of vaginal discharge, with an added drop of normal saline, provides an easy bedside/office test. PCR technology has provided more specific testing and advantage over cultures, which need viable organisms.

The benefits of immediate results mean that the patient has the benefit of treatment on the same day of presentation. Taking a saline mounted slide, for microscopy and immediate result; in addition to ordering PCR test, makes the best use of both tests' advantages.

Genital Human Papilloma Virus (HPV) and genital warts are not a usual cause of pain or dyspareunia; although sub-clinical and small lesions may be associated with irritation and itching, vulvo-vaginitis and Balano-posthitis. The cosmetic and psychological impact perpetuates the patient's distress. Warts may be large and cause a psychological and/or mechanical barrier to intercourse. Trauma, secondary infection and/or inflammation of the warty area, although rare, can add to the patients' distress and Dyspareunia. Treatment modalities (e.g. topical cytotoxics, cryotherapy, chemical cauterisation, electro-cautery, hyfercation and/or LASER) aim to destroy the wart tissue. Most of the patients would have no remaining signs of the lesions, after recovery.

It is not usual for dyspareunia to follow any of the treatment modalities. The immediate post-operative period is associated with pain, due to the subsequent post treatment inflammatory process. An over enthusiastic application or patient's heightened response, to any of the topical applications, may lead to allergic reactions, inflammation, fibrosis, loss of skin elasticity and consequently Dyspareunia. The introduction of vaccination against the oncogenic Human Papilloma Virus (HPV) types is aimed to impact mainly on Cervical Intraepithelial Neoplasia. There are early reports suggesting that there is a reduction impact on genital warts.

Bartholin's Cyst and *abscess* can lead to pain with or without sexual intercourse. The dull aching pain of a cyst will change into a throbbing one with an abscess. The clinician can make a provisional suspicion on history and confirm the diagnosis on clinical assessment. A well-informed patient can make her own diagnosis. Some mild and early cases may settle on antibiotic therapy; but recurrence may take place. Treatment should aim for preservation of the cyst wall; by performing Marsupialisation under general or local anaesthesia. CO_2 LASER incision of the cyst wall to create an opening, provide new alternative management techniques. Treatment should aim to preserve the Bartholin's gland, for its function. Gland excision will reduce vulval lubrication during sexual intercourse and consequently cause dryness and dyspareunia.

Le Peyronie's Disease, its inflammatory penile fibrous plaques of and the consequent and progressive bend and distortion are usually associated with Dyspareunia. The patient experiences pain at the active phase of a progressive disease course. Patients with established condition have less complaints of pain, but are more distressed due to the cosmetic appearance. The penile curvature may be severe enough to contribute to performance problems and Dyspareunia, in either partner.

The male patient's embarrassment could be exacerbated by the reactions of a bemused and/or non-sympathetic female partner. Surgical correction, plaque excision, saphenous vein implants and penile prostheses are alternative options and usually successful in straightening the penile shaft. The condition is more prevalent than previously reported.

Surgical correction is not required in all cases. Medical treatments, oral Colchicine, oral Vitamin E in high dosages, and/or topical injection of steroids or calcium channel blockers into the fibrous bands are used on empirical basis. These treatments lack evidence or comparative studies. Extra corporal shock-wave therapy is showing conflicting outcome results. The long-term effects remain to be identified.

It is important to qualify and quantify the benefits to the patient in terms of cosmetic and functional outcome: (i.e. is it the shape, function or combination that the patient wants? Does the treatment modality address the patient's need?).

E) Allergic Genital Skin Conditions

Allergic Vulvo Vaginitis or Balano-posthitis receive little attention in literature; but a common cause for Dyspareunia. Western countries are experiencing a surge in allergic reactions, due to high and increasing environmental pollution and chemical food additives. The attending clinician should not under-estimate the increasing use of materials, with potential allergens in foods, drinks and skin care. The patient's record of events, a pain diary and elimination of suspected materials should be pursued first. The reported increase in general and specific allergic reactions is bound to reflect on the genital skin.

The initiation of primary or secondary immune reactions in the genital area is perpetuated by local factors. The habitual enclosure and entrapment generated by clothing habits increase the opportunity of genital skin's exposure to allergens. Tight and synthetic underwear, heavy trousers and jeans lead to entrapment of secretions, temperature and humidity and exacerbate the opportunity of the genital skin contact with allergens.

Chemicals, from fabric detergents and skin cleansing soaps and shampoos, are likely to changes the antigenecity of many of these elements, widening the prospect of exposure to numerable antigens and the development of allergic reactions. The vaginal epithelium is unique in ability to produce transudate; as compared to other epithelium, which proactively secretes and/or exclude plasma components. The vaginal transudate exposes the vagina and vulva to a wider host of allergens. The direct contact of these allergens with the genital skin of the sexual partner can also provoke a cascade of allergic reactions. There are reports of genital skin allergy, in patients with history of allergy to a certain drug, following sexual intercourse with a partner who has had the same drug. This suggests the indirect excretion of the drug, into the vaginal transudate and the subsequent exposure of the sex partner. The varieties of allergens, which are produced by innate and/or external factors, open endless possibilities. The identification of causative allergen could prove cumbersome. The recognition of these factors would help to avoid them in the first place and reduce the possibilities of reactions. Skin patch testing, for genital skin allergy, is less frequently practiced, than for other skin allergies.

The keeping a diary of possible agents, by an observant patient, is indispensable. The patient's keeping of a diary for the likely provocative factors could prove helpful in identifying the agent, considering the endless list of allergens. It will narrow the list to the most likely ones. The clinical finding of additional allergic reactions in patients with identified pathology (e.g. Lichen sclerosis), indicates the multi-factorial aetiology of some genital skin conditions that cause dyspareunia.

Addressing one cause only may not achieve the best improvement possible for the patient. Clinical experience suggests that adding an anti-histaminic and anti-allergic therapy, to anti-microbial in the treatment of severe Fungal/Bacterial Vulvitis or Balano-posthitis produces better symptomatic response. Whether allergy is part of the genital skin inflammatory response to infection and whether anti-allergic therapy is of benefit, requires further research.

Establishing whether the allergic reaction is primary or secondary will help to lay grounds for prevention and prophylaxis. The empirical use of topical and systemic anti-allergic therapy is unavoidable in persistent cases; to relief patient symptoms. The introduction of new lines of non-steroidal topical applications (e.g. Tacrolimus, Primecrolimus) widens the prospect of choice of therapy without the anxieties associated with the use of steroidal preparations on genital skin. The cost of these preparations continues to be a practical consideration for long term use. Anecdotal reports suggest a clinical benefit and wider comparative studies are required.

F) Aphthous Genital Ulcerations and Behcet's Disease

Aphthous vulval ulcerations are reported less commonly than the oral ones; although this is likely to be an under-diagnosis. Confirming the diagnosis is important; to establish the right line of management. The ulcerative condition has a protracted course that may extend for weeks; but could be aborted with early diagnosis and treatment. This proves easier in recurrent ulcers. It is important to exclude the possibility of the genital ulcer being herpetic or syphilitic in nature. The history and extent of pain help to differentiate it from syphilitic ulcer, but proactive exclusion of syphilis should be in place. The availability of the Nucleic Acid Amplification Test (NAATs), to confirm or exclude the diagnosis of herpes, gives earlier results than viral cultures. Negative Herpes Serology/ Antibody testing can lend retrospective support in excluding HSV as the cause of the ulcer. The serology test is clinically useful if negative; which indicates no exposure. A positive test may relate to past exposure.

Increasing IgM antibody titers support a current herpetic attack. Aphthous ulcers benefit from the application of potent topical steroid preparations. Topical steroids can worsen the clinical course of herpetic genital ulcerations, hence the necessity for a prudent diagnosis. Antibiotics may be required if there is secondary infection.

Behcet's Disease can cause both genital and oral mucosal ulcerations and relapsing multi-sytem vasculitis. Earlier cases may be clinically misleading, due to the appearance of genital ulcerations with no concomitant systemic conditions. The lack of pathognomonic test for Behcet's Disease and basing the diagnosis on clinical findings imposes a challenge to the clinician; especially when there is full clinical picture. A full-blown disease, with arthritis and uvietis, is associated with generalised pains, which adds to the Dyspareunia that is caused by the genital ulceration. The genital lesion may lead a sub-acute course of several weeks, which perpetuates the patient's distress. In some severe cases, immune- suppressive therapy may be required.

G) Genital tumours

Vulval and penile tumours may rarely present as genital pain and/or dyspareunia. The condition used to affect older patients; but there is marked reduction of age at first presentation. Genital cancers may present with history of Dyspareunia and/or genital pain. Improved health care, longevity and quality of life in later years have reflected on sexual relationships. Changes in sexual relationships and concerns with STIs may bring the patient first to the attention of the genito-urinary clinic. The presentation of genital tumours could be challenging when there is a superimposed inflammation. The inflammatory oedema and/ or erythema may mask the early penile or vulval cancer. The clinical practice of reviewing the patient's condition, after the resolution of the superimposed inflammation, helps to avoid this failure and unmask other pathology (e.g. LS, LP, VIN or PIN). *Testicular Tumours* would usually present with mass and/or ache, rather than Dyspareunia.

H) Genital Conditions with Un-Identified Aetiology

The diagnosis of *Vulvodynia / Vulval Pain Syndromes* (VPS) will depend on the thorough and systematic exclusion of identified pathology and disease conditions. We must recognise that this depends on the body of medical knowledge and clinical expertise that is available to the individual patient, at that point of time. The identification of genital skin burning sensation associated with alcohol and the recognition of a scientific explanation; indicates that what we may consider idiopathic in today's practice may have a plausible explanation with tomorrow's knowledge. The observation of a correlation between genital skin burning sensation and prior consumption of alcohol, cessation of symptoms with abstinence, has a valid scientific explanation. Ethanol lowers the threshold of Vanilloid Receptor-1 (VR 1) for heat activation. VR 1 is heat-gated ion channel that is responsible for the burning sensation. The lowering of heat threshold, from approximately 42°C to 34°C, leads the patient to feel burning sensation at normal body temperature. Another example is the association between caffeine and genital sk9in burning; which has a scientific explanation. Caffeine is a common nervous system stimulant. In laboratory experimentation, caffeine blocked the effect of Amitriptyline in alleviating the hyper-algesia. Caffeine and alcohol association with genital pain should be explored further.

The management of *Vulvodynia* and Vulval Pain Syndromes is progressing with the build-up of clinical expertise. The International Society for the Study of Vulvo Vaginal Disease (ISSVD) recent redefinition of Vulvodynia as "vulval discomfort in the absence of gross anatomic or neurological findings" draws the boundaries of recognition. The pain is conditions subdivided to generalised or localised, provoked or unprovoked. Clinically, a mixture of modalities exists, which requires dynamic management strategy. The process of excluding gross anatomic and/or neurological pathology will require many and recurrent consultations, investigations and treatments. Eventually, the treatment modality of Vulvodynia will eventually depend on the background expertise of the attending doctor. Physicians would usually resort to topical applications like local anaesthetic creams, systemic Antidepressants and/or Anti-convulsants. Physiotherapists resort to biofeedback and physical therapy. Gynaecologists have taken the drastic step of removing the vulval vestibular skin (Vestibulectomy) and others applied LASER treatment to the vestibular area. Most therapeutic reports are anecdotal and single mode trials.

There are few comparative, double blind or placebo-controlled studies. The spectrum of therapeutic modalities for treating Vulvodynia is wide and progressing. There is a new trend to publish comparative studies for different modalities of treatment. Cognitive/behavioural therapy, surface electromyography biofeedback and Vestibulectomy were compared; but the small number of patients undermines any conclusive evidence. The trend of searching and comparing treatments, for the management of Dyspareunia, is a welcomed approach. It lays the principles for practising "Evidence Based Medicine". The studies of molecular physiology and patho-physiology provide a good base for understanding aetiology and developing treatment strategies.

Dysaesthetic Peno-Scroto-Dynia: (DPSD) is the male equivalent of Vulvodynia / Vulval Pain Syndrome. The male patient's presentation, clinical findings and response to modalities of treatment, is similar to patients suffering "Dysaesthetic Vulvodynia".

II) Deep Dyspareunia

A) Pelvic and Lower Abdominal Trauma

The Retro-Verted-Flexed (RVF) uterus may entrap the ovaries into The Pouch of Douglas; by way of positioning. It is a common finding, in some 20% of women. The RVF uterus incarcerates the ovaries into the pouch of Douglas and makes them vulnerable to direct compression and trauma during the thrusting of sexual intercourse. The clinician should suspect the condition from the patient's history. Clinical examination and Ultra-sonography confirm the diagnosis. There need to be awareness of concurrent pathology. Other aetiology of deep dyspareunia should be pro-actively thought and excluded. The mere medical explanation of the condition; and the couple's change of position during sexual intercourse (e.g. woman on top or knee-chest position); usually prove successful, in most cases. Laparoscopic shortening of the round ligament and uterine suspension, to bring the uterine fundus and consequently the ovaries to a forward position, provide a surgical alternative in persistent cases. This option should be reserved to conditions when simple and natural methods fail (e.g. change of position during intercourse). There was a time when the use of vaginal pessaries contributed into the correction of uterine retroversion. There is a place for vaginal pessaries in patients who decline or unsuitable for surgery.

Ectopic pregnancy may present with excruciating pelvic pain. The patient may experience the pain first during sexual intercourse, at the point of rupture of the ectopic sack. A sub-acute and progressive ectopic pregnancy, may be associated with pelvic and/or lower abdominal pain and tenderness, during sexual intercourse. The alarming history of pelvic pain, followed by vaginal bleeding should alarm clinical attention for the diagnosis of ectopic pregnancy and initiate a cascade of medical emergency. A long-standing and sub-acute case of ectopic pregnancy may lead to pelvic fibrosis, recurrent and chronic pelvic pain and Dyspareunia. The increased sensitivity of pregnancy testing, the availability of the Human Chorionic Gonadotrophine (HCG) measurement assays and the better resolution of ultrasonic imaging techniques improved the early diagnosis and treatment of ectopic pregnancy. There continues to be a need for prudent clinical suspicion and tracking of necessary investigations; to make an early diagnosis and timely intervention.

Large uterine fibroids and *ovarian cysts* may be incidentally diagnosed following a complaint of Dyspareunia. Therefore, it should not be presumed that the most prominent or superficial finding is the cause of dyspareunia. A thorough and holistic clinical approach is necessary, to establish the true aetiology; as more than one cause could be encountered.

B) Pelvic and Lower Abdominal Inflammations:

Pelvic Inflammatory Disease (PID) produces variable degrees of Dyspareunia. The pain may range from mild and recurrent attacks to the complete inability to have sexual intercourse. PID, whether acute or chronic, may lead to tubal damage, infertility, ectopic pregnancy and/or chronic pelvic pain. The complications can lead to distress, anxiety, guilt and/or anger; which may aggravate the sense of pain. A high degree of clinical suspicion of PID is required in the differential diagnosis of pelvic pain in woman. We should proactively consider PID in the differential diagnosis of any case of deep Dyspareunia. The delay in processing microbiological samples, coupled with cases diagnosed as "non-specific PID" require the initiation of empirical anti-microbial therapy, at the point of clinical diagnosis to circumvent the sequellae of PID complications. A high Erythrocyte Sedimentation Rate (ESR) and C Reactive Protein (CRP) help to support the diagnosis, retrospectively. The sex partner/s requires investigations, to exclude and treat any concurrent STIs. There is a case for epidemiological treatment for the sex partner. Diagnostic Laparoscopy has a place in the investigations of acute pelvic pain in woman.

The availability of emergency laparoscopy for acute pelvic pain has the benefit of confirming the diagnosis of PID. It provides the best specificity in the diagnostic criteria and is useful in atypical presentations. There will also be a need for a diagnostic laparoscopy, in a patient presenting later with chronic pelvic pain. The early diagnosis of PID and initiation of adequate therapy avoid the long-term sequellae.

Lower abdominal/Pelvic organ disease may present in many ways, including Dyspareunia. Interstitial cystitis, ulcerative colitis, diverticulitis, Crohn's disease and lower abdominal/pelvic tumours are examples. The association of gastrointestinal or urinary symptoms may give a clue for setting a differential diagnosis; but its absence should not preclude considering the conditions in the list of aetiologies. When urinary frequency, urgency and nocturia are associated with dyspareunia and pelvic pain, *interstitial cystitis* should be part of the diagnostic evaluation. The introduction of the pelvic Pain and Urgency/Frequency (PUF) symptoms scale can give a balanced and objective attention to urinary symptoms associated with sexual functions. The ensuing sexual dysfunction in females suffering from interstitial cystitis perpetuates the distress associated with pain.

Ulcerative Colitis is associated with variable degrees of sexual dysfunctions, lower abdominal/pelvic pain and Dyspareunia. The pain may extend to the post-operative period, following surgical interventions. Major surgical procedures, like procto-colectomy and ileo-anal anastomosis, are associated with distress and sexual dysfunctions. The embarrassment of faecal incontinence exaggerates the patient's sense of distress and contributes to sexual dysfunction. A proactive pre-operative consideration of the management care plans is evidently leading to fewer complaints of pelvic pain and/or Dyspareunia, following the surgical procedures. A comparative study of sexuality, in patients who had surgery for ulcerative colitis, before and one year after an ileal-pouch-anal anastomosis, indicated that the majority of patients considered that their sexual life had normalised considerably after surgery.

Crohn's disease is a well-recognised cause of chronic lower abdominal, pelvic pain, dyspareunia and sexual dysfunction. Perineal, vulval and penile lesions are rare but can complicate the problem of Dyspareunia and its management; especially in a patient who had hemi-colectomy. Those on medical treatment may experience regression of the genital lesion. Alternatively, the remaining option is the selective excision of a troublesome genital lesion. Improving the patient's general condition will help to improve sexual functions and the relationship between the couple. Genital Mutilation caused by Crohn's may need genital plastic reconstruction.

Intestinal Diverticular Disease and its consequences of abdominal/pelvic chronic inflammatory process, fibrosis, fistulae, abscess and surgical corrections (e.g. hemi-colectomy) could all be associated with different severities of abdomino-pelvic pain and dyspareunia.

H) Malignant Tumours of Pelvic and Lower Abdominal Organs

Gynaecological malignancies may present with genital tract and/or pelvi-abdominal pain. Not all women undertake cervical screening and a thorough clinical assessment should include history of cervical cytology and inspection of the cervix, including colposcopy and biopsy when indicated. Abdominal examination to exclude ovarian masses is not always productive, especially in the distressed patient.

It is also hampered by obese abdominal wall. Pelvi-abdominal ultrasonography and C_{125} and MRI will help the diagnosis in suspicious cases. A proactive approach to exclude the condition is necessary. There continue to be a delay in the diagnosis of ovarian malignancies. Many patients give history of protracted periods of abdominal/pelvic pain and/or Dyspareunia. Uterine body cancer would usually present in later life with post-menopausal bleeding and should be considered and excluded in this age group.

The clinician should not only be mindful of gynaecological cancers at the outset of the patient's referral, but also later on during a protracted course of investigations and treatment; when the cancer related symptoms may be confused with the pre-existing CPPS.

Male urological malignancies (e.g. prostate or bladder cancer) are usually picked up when the patient presents with haematuria. Unfortunately, there are patients who present late with abdominal pain.

It is common for female or male patients presenting with these tumours to complain of dyspareunia. The management of the tumour will take priority. over Dyspareunia; but should not be addressed as an after thought at a later stage, but proactively planned as part of a holistic care plan. The case is significant in vulvo-vaginal and penile tumours, where deformities have a negative impact on the self image; and when cosmetic reconstruction has a positive role.

The building of clinical expertise in the management of cervical cancer, surgery, radiotherapy and/or chemotherapy; and the management of associated sexual dysfunctions and dyspareunia is a noticeable example of good practice. The skills need to be transferred to the management of other female and male genital and pelvic malignancies. The clinical expertise for a "proactive relationship counselling approach" has a record of positive achievements in cervical cancer and should be replicated in other areas.

I) Chronic Neurological, Skeletal and Muscular Pain Conditions

Myofascial pain may originate from the muscles of the hip region and upper thigh and be associated with Dyspareunia. The medical profession is on a learning curve, regarding the association between muscular and fascial Dysfunctions and Dyspareunia. Pelvic floor muscle imbalance and its association with Vaginismus are promoting the exploration of modalities of physio-therapy and biofeedback.

The presence of inflammatory "trigger points", within skeletal muscles and their ligamentous attachments, lead to the experience of pain; and could be used as a confirmatory sign in identifying the condition. The syndrome should be distinguished from Bursitis, Tendonitis, Hyper-mobility syndromes, Fibromyalgia and Fasciitis.

Neurological problems may provide a plausible explanation, for some of the cases of genital/pelvic pain and Dyspareunia, which previously had unidentified aetiology.

Pudendal Neuralgia, compression and entrapment of the Pudendal nerve, is a recognised cause of perineal and/or genital pain. The decompression and transposition of the Pudendal nerve; and the resulting improvement in over 70% of cases, supports the causation postulate.

Generalised or localised chronic pain conditions are associated with sexual problems; as a reflection of the general pain experienced by the patient. The management of sexual dysfunctions and dyspareunia in these patients' conditions can prove clinically challenging. A multi-disciplinary approach is recommended.

The *autonomic dysfunctions* of *fibromyalgia,* the associated anxiety, depression, fatigue, un-refreshing sleep and gastrointestinal complaints, will all reflect on the couple's sexual activity. The pain in these conditions is one of association rather than causation.

C) Pelvic and Lower Abdominal Conditions with Un-Identified Aetiology

Endometriosis associated pain is usually worse during the menstrual cycle, reaching its highest point after menstruation. The resultant pelvic adhesions and fibrosis are associated with chronic pelvic/abdominal ache, with bouts of exacerbations and superimposed Dyspareunia. Satellites lesions (e.g. vaginal fornix Endometriosis), can cause dyspareunia on their own. The size of the endometriosis lesions should not be underestimated in assessing the patient's complaint of pain. It is not uncommon to find small laparoscopic dots of endometriosis in a patient that is suffering and complaining of exquisite pelvic pain and dyspareunia, out of proportion of the lesions' size. Understandably, multiple myometrial lesions can cause pelvic pain, without revealing themselves to the examiner's eye. The treatment of Endometriosis, with ovarian suppressants, requires intensive clinical management of the ensuing oestrogen deprivation symptoms. Oestrogen deprivation will lead to vaginal dryness, which can also lead to Dyspareunia. The intrauterine use of devices containing progesterones (e.g. Levo-norgesterol releasing intra-uterine system), provides a topical alternative, with less concern of the systemic side effects. Studies suggest its benefits for chronic pelvic pain and dysmenorrhoea.

Irritable bowel syndrome is thought to have links with history of child sexual abuse, and the associated pelvic/ abdominal pain can lead to a general sense of misery, sexual relationships included.

Chronic Pelvic Pain Syndrome (CPPS) in men can lead to crippling and distressing symptoms. The syndrome encompasses a group of patients who were diagnosed in the past as having Prostatitis. It can lead the incumbent to be miserable and not able to enjoy life, including sexual intercourse. This is perpetuated by the experience of deep pelvic pain during and/or after ejaculation. The diagnosis of CPPS recognises the need to deal with the most important aspect of the condition: chronic pain. The psychological reaction formation that ensues leads the patient to make an association between sexual intercourse and pain. The ensuing micturition disorders keep reminding the patient with his condition, leading to more misery.

The Sexual Dysfunction (SD) ranges from loss of desire to Dyspareunia. The introduction of clinical guidelines for recognition, diagnosis and management of CPPS would hopefully lead the medical community to its wide adoption and improvement in clinical management of CPPS. Patient kept "pain scales" and "pain diaries" help to provide some measure of the patient's own prospective of the incapacity, his experience of pain and response to treatment

The *CPPS* typically presents with pain as the predominant complaint (e.g. pelvic, perineal, lower abdominal, rectal, lower back, retro-pubic, testicular and/or penile tip pain); including ejaculatory pain. Discomfort could be significant to the point of interfering with the quality of life. The patient may complains of urinary and/or obstructive micturition symptoms (e.g. frequency, urgency, nocturia, incomplete emptying of bladder and/or abnormal flow). CPPS has no systemic symptoms, but significant psychological morbidity. The condition is either inflammatory or non inflammatory. On examination, the prostate is tender but not swollen or boggy. In inflammatory CPPS, there are leukocytes, but no significant number of bacteria, in the prostatic fluid. Non inflammatory CPPS have a similar clinical picture; but neither bacteria nor leukocytes are present in the prostatic fluid. The underlying aetiology of CPPS may not be defined in retrospect.

It is possible that there is more than one aetiological factor, each leading to similar group of symptoms and signs in what we collectively recognise as CPPS. In some patients, there is evidence of urinary outlet obstructions and/or sympathetic nervous system dysfunctions. Urinary outlet obstruction is identified on urodynamic studies and Cystoscopy. In some patients, there is concurrent interstitial cystitis. In others, there are foreign prostatic antigens and an antigen-antibody reaction is postulated. Pelvic floor muscle dysfunction had been demonstrated in some patients. These findings may be consequences rather than causes of the CPPS. The depressive symptoms and pain intensity predict a poor quality of life, of CPPS patients. We need further data on the correlation between pain, psychological factors and CPPS; to progress and guide our efforts to manage pain.

To date, mono therapy in the treatment of patients with long-term history of CPPS proved to be relatively poor. There are reports of benefits from pelvic floor electromyography, for aiding the diagnosis, and bio-feedback and physio-therapy for management. The reports are interesting but require further long-term analysis on sustainability of benefits. The perspective of considering musculo-skeletal pain, pelvic floor muscular dysfunction, Myofascial pain syndrome and/or functional somatic syndromes as a cause of the pelvic pain will shift the focus from the single diagnosis of chronic Prostatitis into a wider differential diagnosis. There is a recognised therapeutic response to antibiotics; but the anti-inflammatory nature of some of these preparations may have an effect of its own. Attempts to treat the condition with alternative medicine and acupuncture are interesting developments but future progress should include measurable outcome studies.

The Pelvic Congestion Syndrome, also known as *Pelvic Venus Incompetence,* describes chronic pelvic pain in women that is caused by the presence of ovarian and/or pelvic varices; in association with chronic pelvic pain and Dyspareunia. Following the clinical suspicion, Vascular Imaging and Venography help to confirm, or refute, the diagnosis. Transcatheter Selective Embololisation of the iliac veins is reportedly associated with improved pain outcome, in some patients. Different combinations of selective Embolisation, Sclerotherapy and Ligation of Gonadal Veins produced improved results in other reports.

The Nutcracker Syndrome describes compression of the left renal vein, and produces a clinical picture that is similar to that of Pelvic Congestion Syndrome. Endovascular stenting and/or Tran positioning of the left renal vein are alternative treatments, for selective cases when there is confirmation of renal vein compression. The management procedures would benefit from long-term follow-up and outcome assessment studies; to test the relevance of the procedures to the patient's complaint of abdominal/pelvic pain and dyspareunia.

Chapter XVI

Male Chronic Pelvic Pain Syndrome

The male pelvic pain conditions refer to a ubiquitous group of disorders that could be better described under the category of:

- Bacterial Prostatitis:
    - o   Acute Bacterial Prostatitis (ABP)
    - o   Chronic Bacterial Prostatitis (CBP)

- Chronic Pelvic Pain Syndrome (CPPS):
    - o   Inflammatory CPPS; previously called *"Chronic Non-bacterial Prostatitis"*
    - o   Non-inflammatory CPPS; previously called "Prostadodynia"

- Asymptomatic Inflammatory Prostatitis

Bacterial Prostatitis, Acute or Chronic, is usually caused by typical urinary pathogens (e.g. Klebsiella, Proteus, Escherichia coli) and possibly Chlamydia. The route of their entry to the prostate is unknown but possibly through pelvic lymphatic spread. The patient presents with systemic symptoms, pyrexia, rigors, malaise, myalgia and/or arthralgia. A severe ABP condition may progresses to generalised sepsis; with tachycardia, tachypnoea and hypotension. The first presenting symptoms, namely dysuria, frequency and urgency, may be confused with urinary tract infections. The symptoms of prostatitis may or may not be prominent. The typical patient complaint is perineal pain associated with penile tip, lower back or testicular and/or rectal pain. Rectal examination reveal exquisitely tender prostate that is focally or diffusely swollen, warm to touch, boggy and/or indurated.

The symptoms and signs of Chronic Bacterial Prostatitis (CBP) resemble those of Acute Prostatitis but at a milder degree. CBP is the result of recurrent episodes of infection; with or without resolution in-between. The condition of CBP is identified by the recurrent recovery of pathogenic bacteria from prostatic fluid; in the absence of urinary tract infection. The offending organisms are the same as in ABP. Staphylococcus aureus, Streptococcus faecalis and/or Enterococci are also encountered. Chronic infections could be associated by bacteria that were sequestered in the prostatic tissue and therefore not amenable to eradication by antibiotics (e.g. Pseudomonas species, Enterococci, Staphylococcus aureus and rarely Anaerobes).

Chronic Pelvic Pain Syndrome (CPPS)

The CPPS typically presents with pain as the predominant complaint. The pain may be pelvic, perineal, lower abdominal, rectal, lower back, retro-pubic, testicular, penile tip and/or ejaculatory. The discomfort could be significant to the point of interfering with the patient's quality of life. The patient complains of urinary and/or obstructive micturition symptoms (e.g. frequency, urgency, nocturia, incomplete emptying of bladder and/or abnormal flow). There are no systemic symptoms, but significant psychological morbidity. On examination, the prostate is tender but not swollen or boggy.

Inflammatory CPPS is identified by the finding of leukocytes, but no significant number of bacteria, in the prostatic fluid.

Non inflammatory CPPS have a similar clinical picture, but neither bacteria nor leukocytes are present in the prostatic fluid.

The term *Asymptomatic Inflammatory Prostatitis* is reserved for the condition of a patient who has no prostatic symptoms; when leukocytes are encountered, in the prostatic fluid, during the course of investigations. The condition requires careful evaluation, to exclude urethritis, peri-rectal abscess and/or urinary tract infections.

The underlying aetiology of CPPS may not be well defined in retrospect. It is possible that there is more than one aetiological factor, each leading to similar group of symptoms and signs in what we recognise collectively as CPPS. In some patients, there is evidence of urinary outlet obstructions and/or sympathetic nervous system dysfunctions. Urinary outlet obstruction is identified on Urodynamic studies and Cystoscopy. There are CPPS patients with concurrent interstitial cystitis. In others, the finding of foreign prostatic antigen leads to the postulate of an antigen-antibody reaction, as the underlying aetiology. Pelvic floor muscle dysfunction had been demonstrated in some patients. Any of these findings could be consequences rather than causes of CPPS. The recognised therapeutic response of CPPS to antibiotics may suggest a bacterial origin; but the anti-inflammatory nature of some of these antibacterial preparations may have an effect of its own.

Investigations

The process of investigations would be guided by the patient's presentation and/or general condition. In Acute Bacterial Prostatitis, a mid-stream urinalysis is usually positive. Prostatic massage is considered a necessary step in making the diagnosis, in selected cases. The idea of massage of an exquisitely tender prostate will not be acceptable to many patients. The clinician should also consider the possibility of provoking bacteraemia. The practical value is questionable, since the same pathogens are usually isolated from urine. The three urine samples test (i.e. first-void, mid-stream and post-prostatic massage samples) are collected and assessed for microscopy, cultures and antibiotic susceptibility tests. The expressed prostatic secretions could are collected during urethro-cystoscopy. Urinary tract colonization should be excluded, prior to performing the prostatic massage. Post-micturition residual urinary collection in the bladder could be excluded by introducing a course of antimicrobial that does not penetrate the prostatic tissue.

The results that are suggestive of Prostatitis include:

1) Polymorph nuclear cells (PMNL) /High Power Field (HPF) on microscopic examination of Expressed Prostatic Secretions (EPS) or post-massage urine sample.
   PMNL/HPF Ten times or more, than first-void and mid-stream samples are significant
2) Colony count in EPS and post-massage urine sample.

Colonies of more than ten times that of first-void and mid-stream urine samples are significant.

A patient who has a general toxic conditions should have samples for blood culture; prior to any initiation of antibiotic therapy. The aim is to exclude septicaemia and identify antibiotic susceptibility of any cultured organisms, which can guide a review of the antibacterial therapy. Prostatic massage is valuable in afebrile patients and urine samples before and after massage assist the diagnosis. Trans-rectal Ultrasonography is required, to determine the extent of inflammation (e.g. Seminal Vesiculitis), and/or exclude prostatic or para-rectal abscesses. Cystoscopy may be required to exclude other pathology. It may help the diagnosis of urethral outflow obstruction. It could be useful in obtaining trans-urethral samples after prostatic massage, for microbiological investigations.

Treatment of Acute Bacterial Prostatitis (ABP)

The severity and seriousness of ABP requires immediate medical attention and initiation of empirical antibacterial therapy. It may require hospitalisation and parenteral therapy; in severe or non-responsive cases. The clinician needs a low threshold for clinical diagnosis and initiation of prompt antibacterial therapy, to avoid progression to Chronic Bacterial Prostatitis. Samples for microbiological investigations prior to therapy are helpful in guiding the review of treatment; following the antibacterial susceptibility test results. Older patients may suffer urinary retention and a supra-pubic catheter is preferable to a trans-urethral route, to avoid prostatic/urethral damage, bacteraemia and/or septicaemia. In the non-toxic patients, home treatment with oral antibiotic therapy, bed rest, analgesia, and hydration and stool softeners is possible.

Quinolones initial therapy is usually effective. The treatment should continue for at least 28 days; if the clinical response is satisfactory. First line treatment is Ofloxacin (200 mg twice daily) plus Ciprofloxacin (500 mg twice daily), for 28 days. The alternatives include: Norfloxacin (400mg twice daily); all for 28 days. Patients who are allergic to Quinolones could be prescribed Doxycycline (100 mg twice daily), Co-trimoxazole (960 mg twice daily) or Trimethoprim (200 mg twice daily); all for 28 days. The patient would benefit from Non-Steroidal Anti-inflammatory drugs, muscle relaxants (e.g. Cyclobenzapine), Alpha-adrenergic blockers and other symptomatic measures (Sitz-Bath).

In toxic patients, parenteral therapy should be considered, with broad spectrum antibiotics that would affect the likely organisms (e.g. Ampicillin plus Gentamicin). The parenteral treatment should continue until the patient is afebrile for 24-48 hours. The results of the bacterial culture and antibiotic susceptibility test should guide further treatment choice. The initial intravenous antibiotics are followed by oral therapy of Cephalosporins for 4-6 weeks. The success rate of treatment for patients who had equivocal or negative cultures is low.

Patients with ABP who are treated in out-patient require assessment three days after initiation of treatment to review clinical improvement. The patient may need hospitalisation and intravenous antibiotics, if there is deterioration in the clinical condition. A patient with acute bacterial prostatitis requires investigations, after the acute episode, to exclude any underlying abnormalities of the urinary tract. The patient would benefit from urinary tract ultrasonography and possibly intravenous –urogram.

Treatment of Chronic Bacterial Prostatitis (CBP)

The choices include Ciprofloxacin (500 mg, orally, twice daily) or, Ofloxacin (200 mg, orally, twice daily) or, Doxycycline (100 mg, orally, twice daily) or, Trimethoprim (200 mg, orally, twice daily), all for 28 days. There is no evidence that treatment for a longer period with antibiotics provides more benefit.

The diagnosis of Prostatitis is based mainly on symptoms; as signs could be inconclusive. Occult prostatic infection is difficult to exclude. Antibiotic treatment may prove effective due to the anti-inflammatory effect of some drugs (e.g. Tetracyclines). The non-steroidal anti-inflammatory agents have therapeutic benefits, in addition to their symptomatic relief. Lack of response to adequate treatment should raise the suspicion of the possibility of prostatic abscess which may require aspiration, evacuation and drainage. Many Prostatic Abscesses are discovered incidentally, during prostatic surgery or endoscopy; including rupture during instrumentation. Selective Alpha-blockers may prove valuable, if there is evidence of urinary outlet obstruction. The clinical response provides guidance to their continued and long-term use.

The Management of Male Chronic Pelvic Pain Syndrome (CPPS) [Inflammatory and Non-Inflammatory]

The diagnosis of CPPS is made retrospectively, following a history of recurrent episodes. Asking the patient to keep Pain Diary will help the diagnosis; provide a measure of the patient's frequency, severity and duration of symptoms and response to treatment. The patient would usually have had investigations and treatment for prostatitis, including three urine samples tests, pelvic/trans-rectal ultra-sonography, urethro-cystoscopy, prostatic massage, urodynamic studies and/or repeated courses of antibiotics.

The treatment modalities are still under scrutiny. There are reports of benefits, but the patient should be warned of the chronic nature of CPPS and its long term care plane. The following therapeutic options prove valuable: Muscle Relaxants, to counter-act pelvic floor dysfunction, Selective Serotonin Re-uptake Inhibitors (SSRIs), to modulate the perception of pain, pelvic microwave/heat therapy, to induce hyperaemia, Benzodiazepines, to counteract anxiety and/or sacral nerve stimulation, to reverse referred pain. Different combinations of therapy were reported to be beneficial, for selected patients.

Chapter XVII

Female Chronic Pelvic Pain Syndrome

Chronic Pelvic Pain Syndrome (CPPS) in females refers to intermittent or chronic lower abdomen and/or pelvic pain of more than 6 months' duration; that is not exclusively association with intercourse, menstruation and/or pregnancy. The diagnosis is reached by exclusion; following extended assessment and investigations. The clinical analysis of medical history, character and type of pain can direct the management strategy. Menstrual period and cyclical pain is more likely to be gynaecological in nature. The pelvic congestion, associated with the menstrual cycle, may also worsen symptom-complex conditions (e.g. irritable bowel syndrome or pelvic venous congestion). Past pelvic infection, surgery and/or endometriosis are common culprits for adhesions; which are mostly asymptomatic, especially when old and avascular. Vascular adhesions are likely to cause pain, due to stretching from distended adjacent organs, and would benefit from surgical division. Cyclic pain that waxes and wanes with the menstrual cycle may be hormonal. Ovarian suppression, with Gonadotrophin-Rleasing Hormone (GnRH) agonist, is a useful therapeutic test; to confirm the clinical diagnosis, quantify the underlying cause and measure the likely response to surgical treatment (e.g. Oophorectomy). The diagnosis of irritable bowel Syndrome (IBS) relies on precise history taking and patient symptoms. The symptom based diagnostic criteria are reliable and prove accurate on long term follow-up.

Patients with chronic pelvic pain may have a primary musculo-skeletal condition that is causing their symptoms. Additionally, patients with chronic pelvi-abdominal pain may adopt postural alterations that can lead to musculo-skeletal pain. Nerve compression and/or hypoxia will lead to pain, remarkably referred to its course of distribution; whether the compression is due to scar tissue or a naturally narrow passage. Psychosocial factors may be a cause as well as a result of the chronic pain condition and need to be resolved as part of the management strategy. Symptom based questionnaires are valuable for the assessment of psychological co-morbidity. Reports of association between chronic pain conditions and past child sexual abuse (CSA) should be handled with caution. The clinician needs to explore the issue sensitively to direct management; with objectivity in diagnosis and treatment. The wrong diagnosis of CSA would have negative incriminating effect on both the patient and her family.

Laparoscopy is better reserved for confirmation of pelvi-abdominal adhesions and/or endometriosis; especially when fertility is an issue. The patient's anxiety that "something is drastically wrong" perpetuates the pain complex and a negative laparoscopic finding should be proactively used by the clinician to assure the patient to alleviate anxiety. Trans-vaginal ultrasonography scanning and MRI are useful tools for excluding gross pathology; but would not identify many cases of endometriosis or pelvi-abdominal adhesions. Quite often, every additional "negative" test result increases the patient frustrations; due to the lack of explanation of the underlying aetiology of pain. Many women would have had the unpleasant experience and insinuation that it is "all in her head". Others would have gone from one speciality to another with the notion that "nothing is wrong"; with no redress of the patient's main problem of chronic pelvic pain. The multi-disciplinary team approach requires clinical leadership to manage referrals and therapy.

CPPS may co-exist with irritable bowel syndrome or interstitial cystitis which poses a management challenge. Treatment of the bowel or bladder condition alone may not fully alleviate the symptoms. An integrated approach towards managing the CPPS co-morbidities, with a combination of analgesics, psycho-therapy and physio-therapy, should be adopted in parallel with the investigative process which could be protracted. The availability of "pain management clinic" is invaluable in providing psycho-social support and cascading analgesic pharmacotherapy. The drugs should progress from non-steroidal anti-inflammatory agents, Paracetamol and Co-dydramol; before any consideration of opioids.

There is a place for Gabapentin or Pergabalin; when there is clinical evidence of associated neuropathic pain. The decision of using opioids is better undertaken by a clinic committed and charged with its prescription and long term care. Smooth muscle relaxants and antispasmodics (e.g. Mebeverine hydrochloride) have a good efficacy track record in the treatment of IBS, contrary to bulking agents, despite their widespread use. Exclusion of dietary components that contribute to IBS leads to appreciable improvement in symptoms (e.g. grains and dairy products). Ovarian suppression, combined oral contraceptive pill, Levo-norgesterol releasing intrauterine system or GnRH agonist, is a valuable therapeutic test, when used for 3-6 months for the cyclical pain associated with endometriosis or pelvic-venous congestion.

Chapter XVIII

Vulvodynia

Vulvodynia defines vulval pain, discomfort or unpleasant sensations; in the absence of clinically identifiable pathology, whether traumatic, inflammatory, degenerative, immunological, neoplastic, and/or neurological. Depending on the site and spread of pain, Vulvodynia may be Generalised (i.e. affecting the whole vulva), or Localised (e.g. Vestibulodynia or Clitoridynia). The pain and discomfort may be spontaneous and unprovoked or provoked (e.g. on insertion of tampons, intercourse, clinical examination) or mixed. The pain may have existed as long as the patient can remember (i.e. Primary), or after a pain free period (i.e. Secondary). The pain is quantified as mild, moderate or severe; based on the patient's history and findings during the clinical assessment (e.g. cotton bud test). This quantification will help the patient and physician to consider the treatment options and to assess the response to treatment.

The underlying cause of Vulvodynia is widely investigated. There is no one finding that may explain the majority of cases. The finding of more nerve endings in mucosal biopsy samples, undertaken from patients suffering with Vestibulodynia, gives some explanation in a sub-group of patients. It has parallels with the finding of increased nerve endings in interstitial cystitis. Genetic, developmental, metabolic, inflammatory, immunological, hormonal factors were explored and postulated.

The diagnosis is clinical and is usually suggested from the history. Clinical skills, similar to those applied in the investigation of dyspareunia, are required for investigating the case of Vulvodynia. The availability of over the counter medications means that some patients may have had repeated courses of treatments, for what they presume to be vulvo-vaginal candidiasis (VVC), with no permanent cure. Alleviation of symptoms is expected if there had been a concurrent episode of VVC. The clinician should be alert of concurrent conditions, which poses a clinical challenge. The clinician should identify the pain duration, character, spread, provocation and alleviation. History of previous treatments, allergies and/or dermatological conditions is relevant. Medical, surgical history, prescription and non-prescription drugs are recorded for reference and to exclude drug interactions, whilst considering Pharmaco therapy. The emergence of Vulvodynia with superficial dyspareunia and the need to identify "provoked pain" requires the recording of sexual history; which may also open the identification of any associated Sexual Dysfunction (SD). Any associated SD will exaggerate the patient's symptoms and distress. The "Cotton Swab" test is useful in identifying the location and extent of pain and tenderness. There is a place for ruling out concurrent VVC and/or bacterial Vaginosis; which would require treatment before embarking on the management of Vulvodynia. Magnification and illumination (Vulvoscopy) help to identify lesions that may not be identifiable by the naked eye but cause pain that could be interpreted as Vulvodynia (e.g. perineal skin fissures or cracks).

The range and multiplicity of treatments suggests that there is no one single modality that suits every patient or ideal for each case. Topical Anaesthetics do have a place in alleviating pain and distress and could be used on short term or sporadic basis (e.g. before sexual intercourse in provoked Vulvodynia). There are concerns with their long term use and causing sensitisation and allergic reaction; at a later date and distant application (e.g. dental anaesthetics). The clinician should warn the male sexual partner on contact exposure to the topical drugs, during sexual intercourse, which could be managed by using a condom and avoiding oral contact. Lidocaine ointment 5% or Emla cream (Lidocaine 2.5% and Prilocaine 2.5%, Astra Zeneca Pharmaceuticals LP) may be used.

Topical Amitriptyline 2% (Elavel, Astra Zeneca Pharmaceuticals LP) had reports of good response. There is no place for topical anti-fungals, steroids or testosterone. Oestrogen is beneficial in patients with associated post menopausal Vulvo-vaginal atrophy and may have a place in patients with Vestibulities.

Tricyclic antidepressants (e.g. Amitriptyline or Nortriptyline or Desipramine) are common treatments for Vulvodynia and had a long track history. As first line agents, Amitriptyline should start a lower dose of 10-20 mg at night which could then be increased gradually to attain relief. It should not exceed 100 mg daily or stop suddenly. It requires caution and smaller dosage in the elderly.

Guideline management of peripheral neuropathy approve Tricyclic anti-depressants (TCA), Serotonin and nor-epinephrine dual reuptake inhibitors (SNRI) and calcium channel alpha (2) –delta ligands (i.e. Gabapentin and Pergabalin) and/or topical Lidocaine as first line therapy.

Chapter XIX

Peno-Scroto-Dynia

Peno-Scroto-Dynia (PSD) is defined as pain or unpleasant sensation in what otherwise is a normally looking male genital skin and in absence of clinical evidence of pathology or other evidence of "somatisation" of emotional distress. The condition may have an impact on the patient's physical and mental wellbeing. The condition bears similarities to the "Burning Vulva Syndrome", currently defined as "Vulvodynia"; but less well acknowledged due to paucity in literature and low reporting.

PSD could be Generalised, when it affect most of the genital skin or localised (e.g. Scrotodynia), otherwise known as "Red Scrotum Syndrome". The pain could be provoked (e.g. allodynia or hyperaesthesia), unprovoked or mixed. There are benefits in grading the condition as severe, moderate or mild.

Aetiology is masked in most cases. There are cases in association with alcohol and allergy to its metabolic by-products is a possibility. Alternatively, alcohol lowering the Vanilloid receptors threshold for heat activation will trigger a burning sensation at normal temperature. Caffeine is implicated in some cases. The associated hyperaemia and cyanosis suggest a neuro-vascular phenomenon and peripheral micro-vascular arterio-venous shunting of blood (Erythromelalgia). The response to neurotropic drugs and eliciting the pain, in some cases, by pressure on the dorsal nerve of penis suggests a neuropathic aetiology. The exploration of the role of hypothalamic-pituitary-adrenal axis function, Acid Sensing Ion Channels and chemo-electrical transducers, in producing nociception and pain, may shed further explanation.

Penodynia is reported more frequently than scrotodynia; but there is paucity in reporting PSD. Some cases of PSD are associated with stomatodynia.

The clinician needs to make a clear Detailed medical history of PSD may show a link to ingestible materials (e.g. alcohol or caffeine); or contact dermatitis. The removal of the offending agent, in these cases leads to recovery; which helps in supporting the diagnosis. These should be recognised as separate clinical entities from DPSD.

The diagnosis is made on the patient's history, the lack of clinical evidence of pathology and the exclusion and/or treatment of any concurrent condition. There need to be a differential diagnosis with pain of urethritis, orchalgia, penile tip referred pain, deep pelvic pain. Keeping a "Pain Diary" and a record of provoking or precipitating factors help diagnosis and assessment of therapy. Many patients would have had urological investigations (e.g. pelvi-abdominal ultra-sonography, Cysto-urethro-scopy, urodynamic studies...) and tests for STIs, to investigate their symptoms. Examination of the skin under magnification and illumination help to exclude minute lesions. Skin Biopsy is not indicated; unless there is a lesion

Treatment is empirical and would benefit from the learned expertise for the management of "Vulvodynia". Antibiotics, steroids, antifungals and/or antivirals produce no relief. In line with Vulvodynia, the clinician should consider Amitriptyline, Gabapentin, Pergabalain, Carbamazepine or Duloxetine and/or Cognitive Behavioural Therapy. There could be a place for Trans-cutaneous Electrical Nerve Stimulation (TENS).

Chapter XX

Urethral Pain Syndrome

Urethral pain syndrome (UPS) is better reserved for identified cases of persistent or recurrent dysuria, frequency and/or pain and tenderness localised to the urethral region (e.g. localised anterior dyspareunia). It may overlap with Bladder pain syndrome in some cases; but there are patients with clear UPS. The diagnosis is reached by exclusion. The patient may have had the diagnosis and treatment for lower urinary tract infections; when closer investigations indicate that there had never been a culpable organism.

The aetiology had not been defined clearly. There could be evidence of external urethral sphincter over-activity, on urodynamic studies. The patient may also suffer from concurrent pelvic floor muscle over-activity.

Extended three months courses of antibiotics (e.g. Nitrofurantoin or Doxycycline) are effective in some cases; especially those with anti-inflammatory effect. When there is evidence of external urethral sphincter spasm and/or pelvic floor over activity, there is a place for Diazepam, Phenoxybenzamine hydrochloride. Behavioural therapy and voiding retraining should be considered in parallel with pharmacotherapy. Urethrotomy, urethral dilation. and pudendal nerve block. are invasive procedures and should benefit from patient selection Most of the treatments are empirical, with no high level of evidence of efficacy.

Chapter XXI

Bladder Pain Syndrome and Interstitial Cystitis

Bladder Pain Syndrome (BPS) describes the collective symptoms of patients presenting with supra-pubic/ bladder pain, urinary day or night time frequency and urgency. The diagnosis is based on the exclusion of lower genito-urinary acute or chronic infection and benign or malignant tumours. The diagnosis is supported by the finding of bladder sub mucosal haemorrhages, on Cystoscopy. The syndrome applies for symptoms extending for over 12 months; having not responded to antibiotics, urinary antiseptics and/or urinary analgesics. It should exclude those patients who have reduced bladder capacity or suffer with involuntary bladder contractions; which could be identified on urodynamic studies.

There are different hypotheses to explain BPS aetiology. There is evidence of an inflammation and inflammatory infiltrates of plasma cells, lymphocytes and mast cell activation. Non-classic IC though do not show inflammatory cell infiltrates and investigations to date did not elucidate an underlying positive organism. The similarity of some clinical and histological characteristics of IC/BPS to other auto-immune phenomena led scientists to postulate a connection; but studies to date do not show a clear link. One hypothesis postulated that the finding of mucosal cracking, urothelial detachment and defects may be the underlying trigger; which consequently exposes the sub-mucosal nerve filaments and initiates symptoms. There is also evidence of decreased autonomic sympathetic outflow signals; but it is not clear whether this finding a cause or effect. The discovery of decreased bladder blood perfusion, during distension, and reduced micro-vascular density in the sub-urothelium in patients with BPS had led to the hypothesis that tissue hypoxia is the underlying cause. The ability of the urothelium to regenerate, after damage, may well be compromised in these patients. Bladder Urothelium Surface Glycosaminoglycan (GAG) is compromised; allowing urinary chemicals to gain access to the underlying tissues and cause a cycle of inflammation, pain and urinary symptoms. It is postulated that dysfunctional and overactive nerve endings lead to vascular dysfunction and reduced mucosal oxygen supply. The proliferation of nerve fibres, in bladder biopsies of patients with IC, has parallels with similar findings in patients with vestibulities. The aetiology of BPS/IC is most likely multi-factorial.

Epidemiological studies differ on the incidence of BPS/IC in the general population; ranging form 10-400/100,000. BPS/IC is extremely rare in the under-18 years old and relatively uncommon in males. There are indications of a relevant family history in a third of cases. There is a female predominance of about 10:1. A careful clinician would consider the diagnosis of IC in a man presenting with the relevant symptoms; which is sometimes mislabelled as chronic prostatitis. There are associations between BPS and irritable bowel syndrome, fibromyalgia, panic disorders and inflammatory bowel disease. The association with increased autonomic sympathetic over activity is notable in a subgroup of patients presenting with BPS. IC has an association with endometriosis, inflammatory bowel disease and Systemic Lupus Erythematosous.

The diagnosis of BPS/IC is based on clinical symptoms and exclusion of other pathological conditions. The patient would usually have had an extended record of elaborate medical history, physical examination, urinalysis, microscopy and culture tests, urodynamic studies, ultrasonography and post-micturition residual urine volume measurement, Cystoscopy, hydro-distension and bladder wall biopsy. The diagnosis is a chronological and retrospective process that is reached by exclusion. It relies on the clinical, investigative and therapeutic history over the previous year or so. The patient would have had a history of frequent presentations, with lower genito-urinary symptoms, investigations and treatments; but no resolution or relief. The diagnosis is based on the character of supra-pubic/bladder type pain that radiates to the surrounding pelvic organs. The pain increases with bladder filling and is relieved by voiding.

On Cystoscopy, there could be an evidence of a mucosal ulcer, inflammation, scar, new vascularisation and/or reduced bladder capacity. The mucosa of non-ulcerative IC may appear normal initially, on Cystoscopy.

Cystoscopy in a long existing BPS may display sub mucosal haemorrhages, known as "Glamorization".

A biopsy is essential to support the clinical diagnosis of BPS/IC and exclude bladder carcinoma in-situ and tuberculosis. Hydro-distension and Cystoscopy was once considered a gold standard test for the diagnosis of BPS/IC; but need careful consideration as it may contribute to the development of sub-mucosal haemorrhages. A sub-entity of *"Classical Interstitial Cystitis"* is a progressive, destructive, inflammatory condition that leads eventually to a fibrotic small capacity bladder.

The prognosis of BPS/IC is variable and depends on the disease course. The condition may progress to complete resolution; with no recurrences. It may take an intermittent course with waxing and waning; intermittent flares with intervening asymptomatic periods; or the most distressing chronic progressive non-remittent course with increasingly worsening symptoms. The condition has the potential of having a significant and profound effect on the patient's quality of life; particularly with those who have other concurrent chronic pain disorders (e.g. IBS or fibromyalgia).

Treatment Strategies

There is no cure or consistently effective treatment for BPS/ IC; underlined by the fact that the aetiology is not clearly defined. The treatment is mainly symptomatic and supportive. It should be tailored to the patient's own response, as there is no one treatment that suits everyone. There is paucity of research on BPS and IC.

The available studies and publications are hampered by a small number of patients, lack of controlled trials and lack of statistical significance. Some patients observe that some foods and beverages accentuate their symptoms (e.g. alcohol, spices, chocolate and caffeine-containing products, citrus drinks and acidic foods). Some patients report improvement on avoiding these materials; but there is no supportive evidence.

Patients benefit from keeping a pain diary. Bladder training (i.e. clock-managed micturition, on gradual and progressive intervals) has a place, especially when urinary frequency is the main problem. Bladder training does not produce pain improvement; which should be addressed. Some patients make a personal decision to undertake acupuncture and/or hypnotherapy.

A) Pharmacotherapy

Antihistaminic (e.g. Hydroxyzine Hydrochloride), a Histamine H_1 receptor antagonist, and blocks the activation of mast cells provided the basis for its use, in a dosage ranging from 50-75 mg/day. Initial results suggest improvement in symptoms. Amitriptyline, a Tricyclic antidepressant, Acetylcholine receptor blocker, inhibitor of both Serotonin and nor epinephrine reuptake and blocker of Histamine H_1 receptor prove useful in some cases. It is likely that the concomitant anxiolytic effect plays some role. H_2 receptor antagonists (e.g. Cimetidine) proved effective without a good explanation of the likely mechanism of action.

The use of long-term opioids in the management of BPS/IC is a clear proof on the desperate situation that both the patient and the clinician find themselves in; having exhausted all other possible options. The chronic nature of BPS and IC indicates that long-term opioids are only used in exceptional cases and under strict medical supervision. Opioids therapy should be carefully managed and reviewed.

Most patients would have had a presumptive diagnosis of cystitis or lower urinary tract infection on several occasions prior to reaching a definitive diagnosis of BPS/IC. Both patients and clinicians would have realised the uselessness of antibiotic therapy in the management of their condition; except in cases where there is a superimposed UTI, leading to exacerbation of symptoms. The past attempts to use immune-suppressants or corticosteroids in the management of BPS/IC, is a sign of clinician's a desperate attempt to address the patient's distressing symptoms; but have no proven value. The use of neuro-modulators (e.g. Gabapentin or Pregabalin) are widely used for neuropathic pain; and may provide some help; when there is associated peripheral neuropathy (e.g. diabetes or post-herpetic neuralgia)

B) Intra-Vesical Installations

Intra-vesical installation carries the advantages of topical action and avoidance of systemic effects. It requires repeated catheterisation, which is invasive and carries a risk of infection. Local anaesthetics (Lidocaine) results in significant relief of symptoms but requires repetition. Combinations with Heparin and Sodium Bicarbonate are also used. Pentosan Polysulphate Sodium (PPS) is theorised to replenishes the GAG layer with its glycoprotein properties. The studies are limited with small patient numbers, lack of double-blinded controls and long-term follow-ups. Hayluronic Acid bladder installation is based on the idea of repairing the GAG layer defect and seems to reduce the pain symptoms. The frequency of installations ranges from twice to four weekly, depending on the severity of symptoms and response to past modalities of treatment. Dimethyl Sulphoxide (DMSO) ability to penetrate the cell membrane is explored in clinical practice; as anti-inflammatory, analgesic and muscle relaxant. It has become a standard treatment for IC, based initially on empirical trials. DMSO self-installation, twice weekly for 8 weeks, may have a place in a highly motivated patient that is agreeable on self-catheterisation. It should not be used during an episode of UTI. If given for self installation, the clinician should explain clearly to the patient that any suspected episode of UTI should be excluded and treated first. Despite its widespread use by urologists and reported improvements in symptoms by many users, it still requires evidence from large scale double blinded placebo controlled trials. Pentosan-Polysulphate Sodium (PPS) is a glycoprotein that has bladder urothelium coating properties and leads to improvement of symptoms, more notably in classic IC. The effects seem to relate more to the duration of treatment, rather than the daily dosage. Chondroitin sulphate had initial promising results, but awaits further confirmatory trials.

C) Surgical Treatment

Transurethral resection, coagulation and LASER for the Hunner's lesions lead usually to improvement in pain and a reduction in urinary frequency. Relapses may occur in patients having long term follow up. Surgical intervention has no place in non ulcerative BPS/IC.

Cystectomy, ileal conduit and bladder augmentation should be reserved as the last resort for desperate, refractory and longstanding disease. The patient's age, sexual activity, prospects of future pregnancy and possible continuation of associated CPPS symptoms should be weighed carefully during patient selection.

D) Physiotherapy and Psychotherapy

Pelvic floor muscle massage (Thiele massage) and intra-vaginal electrical stimulation are adopted by physiotherapists and may have a place in alleviating concurrent pelvic floor over-activity. There is no scientific evidence of efficacy for either therapy in BPS/IC patients who have no pelvic floor over activity. Trans-cutaneous Electric Nerve Stimulation (TENS) may have a role in conjunction with other therapies.

Chapter XXII

Pudendal Nerve Entrapment

Perineal pain, numbness or burning may be caused by compression or entrapment of the pudendal nerve, in the Ischia-rectal fossa. Clinical suspicion is raised when there is history of unilateral perineal burning sensation that is exacerbated by sitting, relieved by standing and reproduced by unilateral rectal palpation of the ischial spine. The pain could be vague, well-defined, severe or paroxysmal. It may be localised to the perineal and genital area or spread to the lower abdomen, upper thigh or groin. The relevant area becomes sensitive to touch.

Pelvic neuro-genic conditions should be part of the differential diagnosis of pelvic, genital and sexual pain disorders. They could be confused with gynaecological and urological causes of pain; and there are wide areas of overlap. The expertise of a neurologist should be sought if sacral root or conus pathology is suspected.

Temporary Pudendal nerve compression may occur during delivery, as a result of compression of the foetal head against the ischial spine. It can lead to reversible ischemic conduction block. The patient's symptoms appear after delivery and may be masked or confused with other perineal trauma. Spontaneous recovery should be expected, whilst employing analgesics in the interim period.

Neuro-physiological examination requires a neurophysiologist with the right expertise and proves helpful. Pudendal motor latency is measured by the stimulation of the dorsal nerve of the clitoris, whilst recording perineal muscle activity and identifying a delay. MRI investigations may provide diagnostic evidence. Diagnostic nerve block, as a therapeutic test, has a place in confirming the diagnosis and quantifying the benefit of proposed surgical intervention procedures, to decompress the nerve in Alcock's canal. Local nerve block involves injection of a local anaesthetic at the point of maximal hyperalgesia. The subsequent improvement of pain provides a therapeutic test and proof for the underlying causation.

Chapter XXIII

Pelvic Floor Dysfunction

The pelvic floor muscles, in both males and females, play an active part in positioning of the pelvic organs, micturition, defecation and sexual function. They have a role in parturition and may get damaged in the process by untimely, prolonged or precipitous delivery. The medical profession is becoming more aware of pelvic floor muscle laxity, which is associated with pelvic organ prolepses (e.g. cystocoele and/or rectocoele, or uterine prolapse). Milder forms of lax pelvic floor muscles are associated with female urinary stress incontinence; even in the absence of clear physical signs of vaginal wall prolapse.

There is a growing awareness of pelvic floor muscles over activity (e.g. in association with Vaginismus and/or Vulvodynia). In the resting condition, there is a degree of pelvic floor muscle tone and activity; to maintain the integrity of pelvic organs position and function (i.e. urinary and faecal continence). Overactive pelvic floor muscles lead to aching pain; possibly due to compression of the neural and/or vascular supply. Pelvic floor over activity increases afferent neural signals and central nervous system discharge; with a vicious circle of neuro-muscular over activity.

Overactive pelvic floor muscles may present as perineal pain. It could be a widespread and generalised, as part of Vulvodynia, dyspareunia, chronic pelvic pain syndrome, and/or most prominently Vaginismus. Localised pelvic floor muscle over activity produces a hyperactive muscle nodule and *"Myofascial trigger point"*. Although the nodule is localised and hyperirritable; there is considerable pain and muscular dysfunction, in the form of weakness and disrupted relaxation. The condition should be suspected from the patient's history; which is specific. There is history of exaggeration and alleviation of pain, in relation to specific positions and/or movements. The clinician can also identify the muscle nodule during clinical examination (i.e. Trigger Point). The stimulation of the Trigger Point induces pain with the characteristic sensation. Myofascial Trigger Points are not unique to the pelvic floor. Other muscles express similar problems (e.g. gluteal and abdominal wall muscles). The clinician may confirm the diagnosis by injecting a local anaesthetic into the identified Trigger Point, which causes immediate pain relief and relaxation (i.e. therapeutic test).

The management should aim for the alleviation of pain, as well as the improvement of muscular functionality and coordination. Physiotherapy and electro-myography help to demonstrate to the patient the muscular over activity. Electromyography directs the pelvic floor training and relaxation programme. Pressure massage of the Trigger Points promotes muscular relaxation and the consequent alleviation of pain. The patient needs pelvic floor muscle retraining. The detailed regimen of pelvic floor exercise and retraining aims to improve the coordination between the central neural discharge and the peripheral muscular contractility; to reset a more natural and relaxed muscle tone. There had been reported cases of success with Botox intra-muscular injection of the affected muscles; but falls outside its licensing remits. The principal of its use is plausible, on the grounds of notable muscular over activity. It could be considered in association with the physiotherapy and pelvic floor muscle retraining programme, but requires due skill and care on view of rich surrounding vasculature.

Index

A

abuse, 60, 82, 87, 100, 128
access, 17, 166
accounting, 6, 26
accreditation, viii
acetylcholine, 74, 88
acidic, 9, 132, 167
acidity, 9
acne, 33
acromegaly, 91
acupuncture, 145, 167
ADAM, 43
adaptation, vii, 126
adenectomy, 62
adhesions, 131, 143, 153, 154
adjustment, 18, 25, 31
adolescents, 9, 126
adrenal gland, 21, 29, 32
adrenal glands, 21, 29, 32
adulthood, 26, 84
advancement, 99
adverse effects, 31
aetiology, 29, 36, 38, 39, 42, 53, 60, 82, 85,
    90, 112, 113, 114, 115, 118, 120, 123,
    128, 135, 138, 139, 142, 144, 148, 154,
    161, 163, 165, 167
afebrile, 150, 151
affective disorder, 84

Africa, 100
age, 5, 7, 13, 14, 17, 21, 22, 23, 25, 26, 27,
    28, 29, 30, 32, 37, 39, 75, 88, 89, 91, 92,
    97, 110, 136, 141, 169
aging process, 27, 40
agonist, 62, 70, 153, 155
albumin, 31, 32
alcoholism, 5, 24
allergens, 134
allergic reaction, 133, 134, 158
allergy, 123, 134, 161
allergy testing, 123
alpha blocker, 50
alternative medicine, 144
alternative treatments, 145
alters, 91
alveoli, 22
American Psychiatric Association, 118
amputation, 100
amygdala, 14
anabolic steroids, 105
analgesic, 154, 169
anastomosis, 54, 55, 101, 140
anatomy, 124, 128
ancestors, 4
ancient Egyptians, 9
androgen(s), 22, 23, 24, 29, 30, 32, 33, 39,
    74, 75, 84, 90, 91, 92, 105
aneurysm, 97
anger, 139

angina, 47, 51
angiography, 44
angiotensin converting enzyme, 50
angiotensin II, 52
angiotensin receptor blockers, 50
anorgasmia, 57, 62, 76, 90, 93
anoxia, 95
antibiotic, 129, 131, 132, 133, 149, 150,
    151, 168
antibody, 136, 144, 149
antidepressant(s), 51, 74, 75, 76, 93, 96,
    158, 168
antigen, 144, 149
antihypertensive agents, 50
antihypertensive drugs, 51
anti-inflammatory agents, 151, 154
antioxidant, 66
antispasmodics, 155
anus, 3
anxiety, 15, 16, 23, 28, 39, 46, 51, 52, 60,
    61, 62, 65, 66, 70, 78, 82, 84, 88, 95,
    104, 111, 115, 119, 122, 130, 139, 142,
    152, 154
aorta, 98
appetite, 14
arousal, 10, 13, 14, 15, 16, 17, 28, 29, 36,
    58, 59, 60, 61, 74, 75, 79, 82, 85, 90, 92,
    93
arrest, 67
arrhythmia, 47, 48
arteries, 38, 43, 45, 51, 52, 54, 55, 71, 87,
    97
arterioles, 71
artery, 38, 54, 55, 71, 97, 99, 101
arthralgia, 147
arthritis, 30, 136
aspiration, 7, 69, 151
assault, 45, 95
assessment, vii, 23, 24, 31, 32, 33, 40, 41,
    42, 43, 47, 58, 60, 73, 76, 82, 96, 111,
    112, 123, 126, 145, 151, 153, 154, 162
asthma, 24
asymptomatic, 48, 153, 167
atherosclerosis, 55, 87, 97
atmosphere, 40, 52, 119

atrophic vaginitis, 25, 28, 29
atrophy, 26, 28, 29, 66, 74, 76, 97, 126, 128,
    129, 130, 158
attachment, 52
attitudes, ix, 4
authorities, 7, 115
authority, 6
autonomic activity, 119
autonomic nervous system, 16, 87, 104, 106
autonomic neuropathy, 38, 62, 88
aversion, 35, 84, 85
avoidance, 8, 83, 84, 119, 128, 168
awareness, 83, 112, 138, 173

B

bacteria, 144, 148
base, 17, 23, 28, 29, 54, 128, 138
benefits, 3, 33, 40, 67, 79, 121, 125, 132,
    134, 143, 144, 152, 161
benign, 27, 48, 50, 63, 115, 165
benign prostatic hyperplasia, 48, 50
beta blocker, 50
beverages, 167
Bilateral, 32, 95, 98, 131
binding globulin, 44
biofeedback, 83, 137, 138, 142
biopsy, 70, 129, 141, 157, 166, 167
biopsy needle, 70
bipolar disorder, 96
bladder cancer, 141
blame, 7, 41
bleeding, 29, 49, 99, 127, 139, 141
bleeding time, 49
blood, 5, 15, 16, 17, 29, 31, 33, 43, 44, 45,
    49, 50, 53, 54, 69, 70, 71, 87, 89, 101,
    128, 150, 161, 165
blood flow, 15, 16, 45, 50, 69, 71, 89, 101
blood pressure, 16, 17, 43, 49, 51
blood stream, 29
BMI, 38
body image, 84, 85, 95, 97, 98, 99, 100
bone, 21, 22
bone age, 21
bone growth, 22

bowel, 93, 95, 143, 153, 154
bradycardia, 70
brain, 13, 14, 15, 17, 74, 104, 106
breakdown, 111, 129
breast cancer, 30, 84
breast feeding, 9
breathing, 10
buffalo, 11
by-products, 161

C

Ca^{2+}, 52
cabbage, 10
caffeine, 137, 162, 167
calcium, 16, 50, 134, 159
calcium channel blocker, 134
cancer, 29, 30, 31, 97, 98, 100, 136, 141, 142
cancerous cells, 99
candidates, 55
candidiasis, 90, 120, 158
capillary, 38
carcinoma, 167
cardiac arrhythmia, 70
cardiovascular disease, 38, 42, 46, 47, 97
cardiovascular system, 47
Caribbean, 58
caries, 18, 129
castration, 8
catalyst, 18
catheter, 150
Catholic Church, 8
Caucasians, 58
causation, 142, 172
CBP, 147, 148, 151
central nervous system, 90, 111, 173
cervical cancer, 99, 141
cervix, 17, 98, 122, 141
chemical, 133, 134
chemicals, 166
chemotherapy, 24, 29, 74, 84, 141
childhood, 84, 128, 129
children, 5, 7, 8, 28, 62, 81, 99, 129
China, 2, 8

cholinergic medications, 93
chronic diseases, 24, 30
circulation, 15
circumcision, 9, 85, 100, 127, 129
cities, 7
civil servants, 8
clarity, 53
classes, 3, 48
classification, 112, 119, 121
clinical assessment, vii, 23, 32, 39, 74, 84, 93, 120, 121, 133, 141, 157
clinical diagnosis, 83, 122, 126, 128, 131, 139, 150, 153, 167
clinical examination, 43, 82, 122, 157, 174
clinical presentation, 74, 131
clinical symptoms, 93, 166
clinical syndrome, 81, 84
clinical trials, 39, 42, 58, 103
closure, 22, 57, 62, 67, 89
clothing, 134
CNS, 92, 95, 104, 111
CO_2, 133
coagulopathy, 95
cocaine, 39, 69
coercion, ix, 104, 111
colectomy, 140, 141
collagen, 38, 66, 89, 97
colonization, 149
colorectal cancer, 30
communication, 77, 112, 123
community(ies), ix, 8, 37, 114, 120, 143
compensation, 38
competition, 53
complement, 120
complications, 52, 67, 70, 129, 130, 139
compression, 51, 87, 138, 142, 145, 154, 171, 173
conception, 14
conduction, 171
conflict, 82
Confucianism, 3
congestive heart failure, 31, 47
congress, 2
connective tissue, 65, 89, 99
consumption, 137

contact dermatitis, 162
contraceptives, 9
controlled studies, 138
controlled trials, 67, 169
cooperation, vii, 53, 59
coordination, 174
copulation, 17, 59, 100, 126
coronary artery disease, 48
correlation, 26, 38, 119, 123, 137, 144
cortex, 14
corticosteroids, 168
cosmetic, 85, 99, 132, 133, 141
cost, 46, 47, 52, 135
cotton, 157
courtship, 18
crabs, 10
cracks, 41, 130, 158
CRP, 123, 139
cryotherapy, 133
crystallization, 8
CSA, 154
cues, 14
culture, 2, 4, 5, 7, 122, 131, 150, 151, 166
cure, x, 3, 83, 111, 121, 158, 167
cyanosis, 161
cyanotic, 54
cycles, 22, 91, 125
cyst, 133
cystic fibrosis, 24
cystitis, 140, 168
cystoscopy, 149, 152
cytology, 82, 141

D

damages, 96
dancers, 5
danger, 18
death rate, 5
defecation, 7, 94, 173
defects, 165
deficiency, 23, 24, 26, 28, 30, 31, 44, 67,
    73, 74, 76, 82, 91, 125
deflate, 55
deflation, 55

degradation, 105
delusions, 96
dementia, 77, 94
demographic factors, 37
demyelinating disease, 92
denial, 128
deposits, 66
depressants, 33, 39, 60, 62, 63, 104, 115,
    159
depression, 27, 30, 60, 74, 82, 84, 88, 92,
    98, 104, 142
depressive symptoms, 144
deprivation, 24, 28, 143
depth, 51
dermatosis, 82
desire phase, 14
detachment, 165
detergents, 134
diabetes, 30, 32, 33, 38, 42, 43, 44, 46, 48,
    88, 89, 90, 97, 168
diabetic neuropathy, 88, 89, 90
diabetic patients, 31, 38, 88, 89
diagnostic criteria, 132, 140, 153
differential diagnosis, 23, 126, 139, 140,
    144, 162, 171
dilation, 163
disappointment, 15
discomfort, 83, 137, 148, 157
discordance, 74
discrimination, ix, 111
diseases, ix, 9, 11, 46, 48, 112
disgust, 82, 84, 115
disorder, 26, 35, 65, 74, 76, 84, 85, 112
dissatisfaction, 18, 36, 56, 83, 92, 98
dissociation, 110
distillation, 8
distress, x, 26, 57, 58, 71, 73, 82, 84, 98, 99,
    114, 118, 128, 132, 136, 139, 140, 158
distribution, 24, 113, 154
diverticulitis, 140
dizziness, 50, 51, 53
doctors, 111, 120
dominance, 16
donors, 48
dopamine, 14, 17, 51, 62, 74, 105

dopamine agonist, 51, 62, 105
dopamine antagonists, 105
dopaminergic, 57, 62
dosage, 29, 39, 49, 51, 63, 66, 70, 103, 121, 159, 168, 169
dosing, 49
drainage, 70, 96, 128, 151
drawing, 32
drug action, 49
drug interaction, 48, 158
drug side effects, 47, 104, 105
drug therapy, 15, 39, 41, 47
drug treatment, 47, 63
drugs, viii, ix, 9, 24, 33, 39, 46, 48, 49, 51, 59, 60, 62, 69, 74, 75, 76, 77, 83, 91, 104, 105, 106, 116, 151, 154, 158, 161
DSM, 118
dysarthria, 93
dyspareunia, 23, 28, 29, 66, 81, 83, 90, 93, 99, 114, 119, 122, 123, 124, 125, 126, 127, 128, 130, 132, 133, 135, 136, 138, 139, 140, 141, 142, 143, 145, 157, 163, 173
dyspepsia, 48
dysuria, 147, 163

E

East Asia, 39
eastern cultures, 5
ectopic pregnancy, 23, 139
education, 2, 6, 25, 61, 76, 98, 99, 124, 127
Egypt, 1, 4
ejaculation, 3, 9, 17, 21, 23, 24, 38, 43, 54, 57, 58, 59, 60, 61, 62, 63, 89, 93, 95, 96, 104, 115, 143
electrolyte, 70
electromyography, 83, 138, 144
embolism, 30
emergency, 48, 69, 70, 126, 139, 140
emission, 3, 38, 57, 89, 93, 104
emotional distress, 161
emotional experience, 110
empathy, 119
employment, 39

encephalitis, 95
endocrine, 42, 74, 89, 90
endometriosis, 98, 114, 115, 143, 153, 154, 155, 166
endoscopy, 151
endothelial cells, 52
endothelial dysfunction, 97
endothelium, 88
endurance, 18, 43
energy, 1, 6, 43, 96
England, 7
enlargement, 11, 22
entrapment, 83, 84, 131, 134, 142, 171
epidemic, 8
epilepsy, 94, 104
epinephrine, 50, 74, 84, 88, 159, 168
epiphysis, 22
epithelium, 90, 134
EPS, 149
erythrocytosis, 31
ESR, 123, 139
Europe, 7, 8
evacuation, 151
evaporation, 8
evidence, ix, 9, 10, 15, 25, 38, 42, 49, 65, 66, 67, 88, 90, 98, 103, 112, 122, 129, 134, 138, 144, 149, 151, 152, 154, 161, 162, 163, 165, 166, 167, 169, 170, 171
evolution, x
exaggeration, 76, 174
examinations, 115
excision, 55, 67, 98, 133, 140
excitation, 18, 41, 119, 122, 124
exclusion, 37, 42, 136, 137, 153, 162, 163, 165, 166
excretion, 135
exercise, 18, 24, 31, 38, 48, 59, 61, 70, 76, 77, 79, 83, 125, 174
Exhibitionism, x
expertise, viii, x, 23, 40, 41, 85, 137, 141, 162, 171
exploitation, 96
exposure, 24, 55, 59, 126, 131, 134, 136, 158
extracts, 9

F

facial muscles, 16
faecal incontinence, 140
faith, 1
fallopian tubes, 22
families, 7, 8
family history, 166
family life, 5
family planning, 23
fantasy, 14, 60, 61
fascia, 67
fasting, 33, 44
fat, 29
fear, 15, 41, 81, 93, 95, 99, 119
fears, 28
feelings, 14, 77, 111
female partner, 8, 39, 58, 77, 125, 133
fertility, 4, 5, 9, 23, 154
Fetishism, x
fibrin, 66
fibroblasts, 66, 67
fibromyalgia, 142, 166, 167
fibrosis, 23, 40, 52, 53, 56, 70, 71, 82, 83,
     88, 89, 97, 124, 125, 127, 128, 129, 133,
     139, 141, 143
fibrous tissue, 38
financial, 111, 119
financial support, 111
fixation, 126
flexibility, 66
fluid, 15, 70, 85, 144, 148
follicle, 28, 44
follicle stimulating hormone, 28, 44
Follicle Stimulating Hormone (FSH), 21
follicles, 28
food, 10, 15, 134
food additive(s), 134
force, 4, 27
fractures, 95, 127
fresco, 69
Frotteurism, x
fusion, 100

G

gait, 93
gangrene, 126
gel, 54, 59
Gender Dysphoria, x
gender identity, ix
genetic predisposition, 66
genital warts, 132
genitals, 9, 10, 95
ginseng, 10, 50
gland, 22, 133
glucose, 33
Gonadotrophine Releasing Hormone, 21, 91
grading, 132, 161
Greece, 1, 5, 7
Greeks, 6, 9, 10, 69
growth, 9, 21, 22, 24, 131
growth hormone, 24
growth spurt, 21, 22
guidance, vii, 70, 104, 152
guidelines, 104, 143
guilt, 41, 119, 139
guilty, 111

H

habituation, 39
hair, 21, 22, 24, 30
hallucinations, 96
harmful effects, 8
harmony, vii, 4, 14, 119, 125
harvesting, 10
headache, 24, 48, 50, 51
healing, 100
health, ix, 3, 14, 21, 23, 26, 28, 37, 39, 42,
     46, 98, 111, 136
health care, 136
health education, 46
health problems, 3
health promotion, 42
heart rate, 16, 17
height, 17, 24
heroin, 39

herpes, 120, 122, 136
herpes genitalis, 120, 122
high fat, 49
hirsutism, 33, 91
HIV, 30
HLA, 66
HLA-B27, 66
holistic care, 141
homosexuality, 3, 5
hormone, 24, 27, 31, 32, 44, 91, 100
hormone levels, 32
hormones, 32, 90, 92, 105
hospitalization, 96
host, 118, 134
HPV, 132
human, vii, ix, 13, 18, 25, 57, 89, 117
human existence, vii
human experience, ix
humidity, 131, 134
husband, 4, 6
hydrolysis, 48
hygiene, 131
hyperactivity, 24
hypercholesterolemia, 49
hyperplasia, 90
hypersensitivity, 16
hypertension, 39, 42, 46, 47, 51, 65, 67, 70, 87, 97, 103, 104
hypertrophy, 63, 115
hypnotherapy, 83, 167
hypogonadism, 23, 43, 44, 50, 60
hypotension, 48, 147
hypothalamus, 14, 21
hypothesis, 165
hypothyroidism, 74
hypoxia, 97, 154, 166
hysterectomy, 27, 29, 98

I

iatrogenic, 29, 104
ideal, 3, 112, 158
identification, 14, 106, 114, 116, 123, 129, 130, 135, 137, 158
ideology, 7
idiopathic, 137
idiosyncratic, 14
illumination, 158, 162
image, 84, 95, 98, 99, 100, 141
imagery, 75
imagination, 2
immune reaction, 134
impaired immune function, 96
impairments, 45
implants, 29, 33, 70, 100, 133
impotence, 8, 9, 25, 39, 46, 69, 87, 88, 89, 90, 91, 93, 104, 106, 127
improvements, 21, 25, 28, 169
impulses, 50
incidence, 58, 65, 129, 166
independence, 54
index case, 127
India, 1
indirect effect, 29
individuals, vii, 13, 15, 16, 17, 36, 90, 118, 127
induction, 66
industry, 27
infarction, 47
infection, 56, 125, 128, 129, 130, 131, 133, 135, 136, 148, 151, 153, 165, 168
infertility, ix, 139
inflammation, 24, 28, 66, 99, 111, 113, 120, 122, 125, 128, 129, 133, 136, 150, 165, 166
inflammatory bowel disease, 24, 166
inflation, 55
informed consent, 33, 128
inguinal, 113
inheritance, 4
inhibition, 52, 67
inhibitor, 48, 49, 50, 52, 168
initiation, 33, 74, 76, 98, 129, 134, 139, 150, 151
injections, 51, 52, 67
injuries, 48, 55, 95, 125
injury, 87, 88, 95, 97, 98, 125
insecurity, 40
insertion, 29, 47, 54, 78, 113, 126, 127, 157
insomnia, 29, 104

instinct, 2
institutions, 105
integrity, 27, 43, 87, 103, 173
intercourse, 2, 3, 5, 16, 17, 27, 28, 33, 36,
    41, 46, 52, 58, 77, 78, 81, 88, 93, 94, 95,
    100, 113, 114, 115, 124, 130, 132, 133,
    138, 139, 143, 153, 157, 158
interference, 128, 132
interpersonal conflict(s), 58
interpersonal relations, vii, 2, 14, 36, 39, 75,
    96, 112
interpersonal relationships, 2, 14, 96, 112
interstitial cystitis, 123, 140, 144, 149, 154,
    157
intervention, 38, 116, 139, 169
intestine, 9
intimacy, vii, viii, ix, 13, 14, 18, 77, 78, 82,
    84, 111, 125
intoxication, 127
intravenous antibiotics, 151
iron, 10
irrigation, 69
irritable bowel syndrome, 153, 154, 166
ischemia, 54, 70, 97
isolation, 118
issues, vii, 6, 23, 29, 74, 82, 84, 94

K

kidney, 40
kidney failure, 40
kill, 9
Kinsey, 117
kinship, 4
KOH, 132

L

laceration, 71
lack of control, 167
laparoscopic surgery, 98
laparoscopy, 121, 140
latency, 171
later life, 67, 141

laws, 8
LDL, 49
leadership, 154
leakage, 54, 87, 97
learning, 18, 142
legislation, 127
legs, 4, 100
lesions, 95, 96, 121, 122, 129, 130, 132,
    140, 143, 158, 162, 169
leukocytes, 144, 148
levator, 82
libido, 24, 26, 29, 30, 31, 43, 76, 90, 91, 93,
    94, 96, 104, 105
life expectancy, 25
lifestyle changes, 46
ligament, 138
light, 100
linen, 9
lipids, 33
lipoproteins, 49
literacy, 6
longevity, 25, 136
loss of libido, 24, 26, 27, 28, 77, 93, 95, 96
love, 1, 4, 5, 7, 10, 11, 14, 18
low risk, 47
Luteinising Hormone (LH), 21
luteinizing hormone, 28, 44
lying, 15
lymph, 62, 99, 100, 128
lymph node, 99
lymphocytes, 66, 165

M

majority, 16, 17, 38, 46, 96, 127, 140, 157
malaise, 147
malignancy, 120
malnutrition, 24
man, 2, 3, 4, 7, 8, 11, 24, 39, 42, 44, 57, 59,
    60, 61, 88, 126, 166
manic, 51
manic symptoms, 51
manipulation, 95
marijuana, 39, 69, 105
marital conflict, 75

marriage, 2, 4, 5, 8, 81, 115, 117
Masochism, x
mass, 38, 136
mast cells, 168
mastectomy, 84, 100
materials, 9, 134, 162, 167
matrix, 66
matter, iv, 1, 76, 79
maturation process, 21
measurement, 30, 33, 44, 123, 139, 166
measurements, 33
medical, ix, 4, 25, 37, 39, 41, 47, 48, 50, 58,
    65, 69, 73, 82, 85, 104, 110, 112, 114,
    116, 117, 118, 124, 126, 127, 130, 137,
    138, 139, 140, 142, 143, 150, 153, 162,
    166, 168, 173
medical assistance, 47, 73
medical care, 4, 25, 65
medical history, 41, 50, 130, 153, 162, 166
medication, viii, 43, 48
medicine, 132
mellitus, 38, 44, 88
memory, 14, 128
menarche, 22, 28
menopause, 21, 26, 27, 28, 32, 92, 98
menstruation, 28, 143, 153
mental disorder, 118
mental fantasising, 14
Metabolic, 38
metabolic syndrome, 30, 38, 42
metabolism, 32, 49
metals, 11
metatarsal, 43
methadone, 39
methodology, 37
microscopy, 62, 132, 149, 166
Middle East, 8, 10, 58
models, 88
morality, 23
morbidity, 37, 115, 144, 148, 154
motivation, 14, 53
MRI, 141, 154, 171
mucosa, 166
mucus, 15
multiple myeloma, 48

multiple sclerosis, 48
muscle contraction, 81, 115
muscle mass, 24, 30, 169
muscle relaxant, 151, 155, 169
muscle spasms, 81
muscle strength, 76
muscles, 4, 10, 17, 57, 75, 76, 82, 87, 95,
    124, 142, 173, 174
musicians, 5
mutilation, 85, 100, 127
myalgia, 147
myocardial infarction, 47, 48, 49, 51

N

narcotics, 76
nausea, 50, 51
necrosis, 55, 126
negative effects, 15, 49, 100
nerve, 48, 49, 50, 53, 83, 88, 97, 113, 142,
    152, 157, 161, 163, 165, 171
nervous system, 90, 137
neural network, 14
neuralgia, 113, 116, 168
neurologist, 171
neuropathic pain, 82, 83, 154, 168
neuropathy, 38, 88, 89
neuropraxia, 97
neurotransmitters, 14, 38, 74
neutral, 14
nitrates, 49, 51
nitrous oxide, 48, 74
nobility, 4
nocturia, 114, 140, 144, 148
normal development, 67
nuclei, 95
nucleus, 14
nutrition, 21

O

obesity, 24, 32, 38
objectivity, 74, 154
obstruction, 48, 63, 126, 144, 149, 150, 152

occlusion, 38, 51, 97
oedema, 70, 100, 128, 136
oil, 9, 11
oophorectomy, 27, 29, 32, 33, 74, 92
opiates, 74, 75, 105
opioids, 154, 168
opportunities, 8
oral antibiotic, 150
oral lesion, 129
organ, 98, 140, 173
organism, 122, 131, 163, 165
organs, 11, 21, 26, 57, 103, 153, 166, 173
orgasm, 13, 16, 17, 18, 27, 28, 33, 36, 47,
    57, 60, 69, 73, 75, 76, 78, 90, 93, 95, 115
osteoporosis, 29, 30
ovarian cysts, 139
ovaries, 32, 122, 138
overlap, 81, 83, 113, 114, 163, 171
ovulation, 22
ovum, 3
oxygen, 70, 166

P

Paedophilia, x
pain management, 154
palpation, 171
panic disorder, 166
parallel, 26, 51, 59, 84, 113, 122, 154, 163
paralysis, 9, 62, 83, 93
parents, 7, 23
pathogens, 147, 149
pathology, 88, 112, 113, 114, 115, 116, 118,
    121, 123, 128, 130, 135, 136, 137, 138,
    150, 154, 157, 161, 162, 171
patient care, 40
PCR, 131, 132
PDEs, 48
pelvic floor, 4, 17, 27, 28, 57, 60, 76, 81,
    83, 84, 95, 115, 124, 144, 152, 163, 169,
    173, 174
pelvic inflammatory disease, 23, 114
penis, 9, 10, 17, 54, 55, 58, 59, 65, 69, 70,
    78, 88, 124, 127, 161
peptide, 74

perfusion, 166
perineum, 87
peripheral neuropathy, 159, 168
peripheral vascular disease, 54
permission, 74
permit, 37
personal relations, 75
personal relationship, 75
personality, 82, 127
personality disorder, 82
persuasion, 16
petechiae, 54
pharmacotherapy, viii, 46, 47, 94, 116, 154,
    163
phobia, 84, 85, 115
phosphate, 48
photographs, 66
physical activity, 38
physical interaction, 1
physical therapy, 137
physical touching, 14
physicians, viii, 122
physiology, 89, 138
pigmentation, 54
placebo, 29, 62, 67, 92, 138, 169
plants, 11
plaque, 65, 66, 67, 133
plasma cells, 66, 165
plasma levels, 49
plasma proteins, 32
platform, 123
playing, 78
pleasure, ix, 5, 16, 18, 75, 77, 78, 79, 95,
    115, 127
plexus, 97, 98
policy, 121
politics, 6
pollution, 134
population, 15, 30, 65, 88, 166
postural hypotension, 48
predictability, 18
pregnancy, 9, 22, 99, 120, 125, 132, 139,
    153, 169
preparation, iv, 29, 31
prepuce, 128, 129

prescription drugs, 46, 75, 158
preservation, 100, 133
prevention, 13, 46, 135
priapism, 88
primary function, 9
principles, 45, 111, 138
private affair, 1
progesterone, 28, 29, 74, 94
prognosis, 96, 167
prolactin, 31, 32, 44, 90, 91, 105
prolapse, 98, 99, 173
proliferation, 22, 166
prophylaxis, 135
proposition, 82
prostatectomy, 49, 62, 96, 97
prostatitis, 58, 63, 115, 120, 148, 151, 152, 166
prostheses, 55, 56, 126, 133
prosthesis, 11, 37, 42, 55, 56, 66, 67, 71
protection, 23, 124
psychiatric disorders, 51, 75, 127
psychiatrist, 96
psychological functions, 117
psychological problems, 47
psychosis, 96, 104
psychotherapy, 76, 82, 84, 85, 96
pubertal development, 22
puberty, 8, 21, 22, 23, 24, 26
public figures, 8
pumps, 127
punishment, 4
pyogenic, 130

Q

quality of life, 25, 37, 39, 40, 98, 114, 136, 144, 148, 167
quantification, 112, 157
questionnaire, 42, 43

R

race, 39
radiation, 97
radio, 45, 99, 100
radiotherapy, 24, 29, 40, 82, 83, 97, 99, 141
rape, 5, 7, 45, 85
reaction formation, 143
reactions, 14, 77, 82, 84, 111, 125, 133, 134
reading, 60, 77
reality, 92
reasoning, 123
receptors, 32, 91, 104, 111, 161
recognition, 37, 111, 112, 113, 114, 116, 118, 119, 135, 137, 143
recommendations, 3
reconstruction, 67, 126, 127, 141
recovery, 97, 131, 133, 148, 162, 171
recreational, ix, 39, 46, 48, 49, 74, 75, 76, 91
recurrence, 33, 36, 131, 133
reflexes, 75, 93
regenerate, 166
regression, 24, 140
regulations, 22
rehabilitation, 40, 49, 67, 84, 95, 97, 99, 100
rehabilitation program, 84
rejection, 18
relatives, 6
relaxation, 10, 18, 36, 38, 39, 50, 51, 57, 77, 83, 89, 122, 124, 173, 174
relevance, 120, 145
relief, 98, 99, 122, 135, 151, 158, 162, 166, 168, 174
religious beliefs, 2
renal failure, 48
repair, 23, 66, 97
reproduction, ix
repulsion, 84, 132
reputation, 10
requirements, 40
resection, 55, 169
resistance, 28
resolution, vii, viii, 13, 15, 17, 18, 28, 75, 121, 123, 125, 136, 139, 148, 166, 167
respiratory rate, 15, 16
responsiveness, 31, 39, 50, 53, 74
restoration, 24
retrograde ejaculation, 57, 89, 93

rheumatoid arthritis, 24
rhinitis, 48
rights, 5, 111
rings, 3, 39
risk(s), 18, 22, 23, 29, 30, 38, 46, 47, 48, 49,
    52, 53, 55, 65, 66, 71, 97, 98, 112, 119,
    128, 168
risk factors, 30, 38, 65
rodents, 66
root(s), 9, 10, 83, 114, 119, 171
routes, viii
rubber, 54, 127
rules, viii, 2, 104

S

sadness, 43
safety, 7, 33, 46, 53
salpingo-oophorectomy, 98
scar tissue, 65, 154
scarcity, 32, 124
schizophrenia, 96
scientific knowledge, 103
scientific observation, 112, 118
scientific understanding, ix
sclerosis, 43, 89, 92, 125, 128, 129, 131,
    135
scope, x, 30
scrotal, 15, 22, 55, 96, 100, 115, 126
scrotum, 3, 17, 21
secondary sexual characteristics, 24, 26, 43
secretion, 15, 21, 26, 29, 52, 90, 91
sedatives, 104
seizure, 94
self-confidence, 83
self-esteem, 84, 96
self-identity, 127
self-image, 93
semen, 3, 9, 17, 27, 62, 132
seminal vesicle, 22, 63
seminiferous tubules, 89
sensation(s), 55, 78, 90, 93, 99, 113, 132,
    137, 157, 161, 171, 174
sensitivity, 16, 21, 22, 27, 30, 74, 82, 93,
    103, 131, 139

sensory symptoms, 93
sepsis, 147
serology, 136
serotonin, 17, 50, 74
Sertoli cells, 90
serum, 28, 32, 91
services, 7
sex, ix, 1, 3, 4, 5, 8, 10, 14, 15, 17, 18, 22,
    26, 27, 28, 39, 44, 58, 73, 74, 76, 77, 82,
    84, 88, 95, 99, 100, 103, 105, 111, 112,
    117, 124, 125, 130, 132, 135, 139
sex hormones, 8, 26, 74
sex offenders, 105
sexual abuse, 42, 82, 85, 128, 143, 154
sexual activity, 13, 14, 25, 29, 47, 49, 51,
    61, 73, 74, 76, 90, 94, 96, 105, 142, 169
sexual behaviour, ix, 4, 14, 62, 84, 95, 103,
    105, 117, 127, 128
sexual desire, ix, 14, 15, 26, 27, 29, 33, 35,
    36, 43, 47, 58, 73, 74, 85, 92, 94, 104,
    105, 106
Sexual desire in women, 26
sexual dysfunctions, viii, 16, 28, 36, 76, 85,
    90, 96, 100, 103, 104, 111, 140, 142
sexual experiences, 16, 73
sexual health, ix, 23, 111
sexual intercourse, ix, 1, 3, 9, 11, 18, 22, 37,
    46, 47, 51, 54, 55, 60, 66, 76, 77, 78, 81,
    85, 95, 100, 112, 115, 124, 125, 126,
    127, 128, 132, 133, 134, 138, 139, 143,
    158
sexual orientation, 60
sexual problems, 142
Sexual Sadism, x
sexuality, ix, 1, 18, 76, 77, 83, 84, 93, 94,
    95, 111, 140
sexually transmitted infections, 7, 22, 44
shape, 129, 134
shock, 95, 134
showing, 51, 134
sickle cell, 48, 70
side effects, 31, 33, 51, 60, 76, 91, 94, 103,
    105, 116, 143
signals, 13, 83, 165, 173

signs, 31, 93, 112, 122, 133, 144, 148, 149, 151, 173
skeletal muscle, 142
skin, 15, 29, 41, 54, 99, 114, 121, 122, 124, 125, 128, 129, 130, 131, 133, 134, 137, 158, 161, 162
slaves, 5
smoking, 38, 42, 97
smooth muscle, 38, 48, 50, 51, 52, 89, 97, 104, 106
social behaviour, 93
social class, 2
social interactions, 6
social problems, 39
social status, ix, 4, 6
social support, 154
society, vii, 1, 2, 3, 4, 5, 7, 25, 104
Socrates, 6
solution, 70
South America, 9
spasticity, 93, 95
specialisation, x
specialists, 24
species, 148
sperm, 17, 96
sperm function, 96
spermatogenesis, 22, 24, 90
sphincter, 57, 75, 163
spinal cord, 14, 48, 57, 62, 75, 93, 95, 104, 106
spinal cord injury, 62, 75, 95
spine, 171
spontaneity, 79
stability, 67
stable angina, 47
state, ix, 3, 5, 22, 30, 39, 55, 69, 74, 94
state laws, 22
status epilepticus, 94
stenosis, 27
sterilisation, 99
steroids, 14, 21, 28, 32, 121, 130, 134, 136, 158, 162
stimulant, 137

stimulation, 5, 13, 14, 15, 16, 21, 22, 27, 28, 51, 52, 55, 58, 59, 61, 69, 71, 74, 75, 76, 84, 111, 127, 152, 169, 171, 174
stimulus, 15, 84
storage, 9
stress, 16, 48, 81, 88, 111, 119, 173
stress test, 48
stretching, 41, 124, 153
stroke, 48
stroma, 29
structural changes, 88
style, 39
success rate, 67, 151
supervision, viii, 48, 52, 53, 168
suppliers, 49
suppression, 95, 153, 155
surgical intervention, 66, 70, 140, 172
surgical technique, 54, 55, 67
survival, 37, 40
susceptibility, 149, 150, 151
sustainability, 144
sweat, 17, 22
swelling, 11, 15, 74
sympathetic nervous system, 89, 144, 149
sympathy, 119
symptomatic treatment, 83, 119, 120
symptoms, 29, 30, 31, 33, 36, 39, 48, 98, 112, 114, 115, 116, 121, 122, 123, 135, 137, 140, 141, 143, 144, 147, 148, 149, 151, 152, 153, 154, 155, 158, 162, 165, 166, 167, 168, 169, 171
synchronization, 41
syndrome, 38, 77, 91, 95, 112, 114, 142, 143, 144, 163, 165, 173
synthesis, 38, 66, 105
syphilis, 9, 11, 136
syphilitic ulcer, 136

T

tachycardia, 51, 70, 147
target, 61
taxes, 7
techniques, 3, 10, 55, 56, 70, 76, 98, 124, 126, 133, 139

technology, 121, 132
temperature, 96, 131, 134, 137, 161
tension(s), 15, 16, 17, 18, 41, 52, 53, 78, 82
territorial, 112
territory, x, 39
testicle, 126
testicular torsion, 126
testing, 44, 69, 132, 135, 136, 139
testosterone, 14, 15, 21, 24, 26, 29, 30, 31,
    32, 33, 44, 50, 67, 74, 89, 90, 91, 104,
    105, 158
Testosterone Replacement Therapy (TRT),
    24, 26, 30
therapeutic benefits, 151
therapeutic effects, 43
therapeutics, 16, 96, 103, 105
therapist, 18, 59, 79
thiazide, 60, 62
thiazide diuretics, 60, 62
thinning, 125
thoughts, 10, 14, 15
thyroid, 32, 89
thyroxin, 44
time constraints, 42
tissue, 28, 38, 40, 45, 51, 52, 66, 83, 87, 88,
    89, 97, 110, 111, 118, 133, 148, 149, 166
tissue degeneration, 97
tobacco, 87
torsion, 24, 126
toxic effect, 105
toxicity, 8
toys, 10
trainees, 121
training, viii, 51, 99, 167, 174
tranquilizers, 104
transmission, 11, 130
transplant, 101
trauma, 42, 46, 50, 53, 54, 66, 71, 88, 95,
    100, 124, 125, 126, 128, 138, 171
treatment methods, 56
trial, 6
trigeminal neuralgia, 93
tuberculosis, 167
tumours, 24, 55, 126, 136, 140, 141, 165

U

UK, ii, 111
ulcer, 136, 166
ulcerative colitis, 140
ultrasonography, 45, 66, 123, 141, 151, 154,
    166
unstable angina, 47
urethra, 57, 62, 89
urethritis, 132, 148, 162
urinalysis, 44, 149, 166
urinary retention, 150
urinary tract, ix, 29, 39, 96, 123, 148, 151,
    163, 168
urinary tract infection, 96, 148, 163, 168
urine, 8, 9, 62, 149, 150, 152, 166
urothelium, 166, 169
uterine cancer, 29
uterine fibroids, 139
uterine prolapse, 173
uterus, 17, 22, 122, 138

V

vacuum, 46, 54
vagina, 9, 10, 11, 16, 17, 22, 28, 61, 99,
    126, 129, 134
vaginitis, 26, 29, 120, 129, 132
valve, 47
variables, 103, 118
variations, 1, 8, 14
varieties, 29, 135
vascular diseases, 38
vascular occlusion, 44
vascular system, 87
vasculature, 103, 174
vasculitis, 136
vasectomy, 115
vein, 55, 70, 133, 145
venous insufficiency, 87
ventro-medial nucleus (VMN), 14
venules, 89
Venus, 5, 55, 114, 145
vertebrae, 9

vessels, 38, 40, 89
violence, 111
viscosity, 87
visual stimulus, 14
voiding, 163, 166
vulnerability, 23, 124, 125, 128
vulva, 22, 41, 112, 113, 117, 128, 129, 134,
    157
vulval pain, 113, 157
vulvitis, 82, 120

weakness, 9, 76, 83, 173
wealth, 2
websites, 113
well-being, 127
wells, 5
Western countries, 134
white matter, 92
withdrawal, 16, 33
wood, 11
World Health Organisation (WHO), ix
worldwide, 37
wound healing, 65

W

war, 4
warts, 133
waste, 11
water, 5

Y

yang, 9
young women, 23